BEYOND THE
NEXT WAVE

"I have read *Beyond the Next Wave* with great interest and there is no doubt that Glen Peters touches on a major lacuna in British business, particularly small- and medium-sized businesses. Few enough of them have clear goals about where they are aiming and even fewer are 'aiming ahead.' Since it takes quite a long time to change any business organisation it is of the greatest possible importance that you are heading for where business is going to be, rather than where it is at present. Futurology has managed to achieve a rather dubious name amongst businessmen. The fact is that despite the size and inertia of the system the clues to the future lie very much around what is happening today.

Glen Peters' book can only be of help if it achieves a wide circulation – I hope it will."

SIR JOHN HARVEY-JONES MBE

*"A highly intelligent set of
speculations about the future
of doing business. They do not
all have to be right to be
of immense value."*

MARTIN SORRELL,
CEO, WPP Group plc.

about the author

Glen Peters is a partner at Price Waterhouse in London, responsible for identifying future global trends affecting the firm and its clients. He has conducted numerous interviews and "futures" workshops to prove the viability of scenario planning as an aid to product innovation. An engineer by first degree and a PhD in the Management Sciences, he has operated across several industry sectors. He has been formerly responsible for the Market and Customer Management practice and Petroleum Consulting group at Price Waterhouse and has set up an alliance of 50 European companies to benchmark customer management practices.

BEYOND THE NEXT WAVE

imagining the next generation of customers

Glen Peters

London · Hong Kong · Johannesburg
Melbourne · Singapore · Washington DC

PITMAN PUBLISHING
128 Long Acre, London WC2E 9AN
Tel: +44 (0)171 447 2000
Fax: +44 (0)171 240 5771

A Division of Pearson Professional Limited

First published in Great Britain in 1996

© Pearson Professional Limited 1996

The right of Glen Peters to be identified as author
of this work has been asserted by him in accordance
with the Copyright, Designs and Patents Act 1988.

ISBN 0 273 62417 2

British Library Cataloguing in Publication Data
A CIP catalog record for this book can be obtained from the British Library.

10 9 8 7 6 5 4 3 2 1

Typeset by Northern Phototypesetting Co Ltd, Bolton
Printed and bound in Great Britain by Bell & Bain Ltd, Glasgow

The Publishers' policy is to use paper manufactured from sustainable forests.

contents

part one
THE BUSINESS FUTURIST – A NEW COMPETENCE

part two
THE VECTORS OF CHANGE

part three
TWO SCENARIOS FOR 2015

part four
HOW TO DEVELOP SCENARIOS

foreword

Over the years many futurists have worked towards lifting managers' sights up from the day-to-day towards the horizon. However, Pierre Wack, the founder of scenario planning in Shell, was the first to bring to the commercial world an approach and philosophy that has stood the test of time. In the mid-60's, when he set out on this journey, his message was not an easy one. He invited managers to give up the false sense of security, embodied in one forecasted future, and to get used to living with multiple, equally plausible futures in their decision making. The rewards he promised were fundamental, a shift in thinking, and therefore in corporate performance, from reactive to creative.

There was no doubt in Shell that he delivered on his promise. In 1980 Managing Director Andre Bernard wrote in the Harvard Business Review; "Experience has taught us that the scenario technique is much more conducive to forcing people to think about the future than the forecasting techniques we formerly used." I am pleased to have been able to work under Pierre, and eventually step in his footsteps to lead a team of my own. Today, with increasing turbulance and complexity in the organisationl context making traditional economic an market forecasting obsolete, scenario planning is experiencing an exponential explosion in acceptance and popularity.

Glen Peters' book is a powerful new resource for the many scenario planners around the world, both new and experienced. Its focus on the customer of the future and its wide-ranging approach places it in the category known as exploratory scenarios, providing "engines for innovation" without which no organisation can survive today. A significant part of my own research today is devoted to "customer concept engineering", a term we have created to describe the work carried out in relation to developing an understanding of the way customers will evolve in the future. It is this concept from which the successful companies of the next century will build their product and service strategies.

It is a documented fact that managers do not devote a lot of time to jointly envisioning the future. Managers who have been in a line management job for more than 5 years, particularly in successful organisations, tend to lose track of their customers' value systems and how these may evolve. The job of regaining this understanding clearly cannot be farmed out. Managers need to take time out to challenge all their old preconceptions about their market and in this way become open to new ideas and influences as these emerge.

The forces of change affecting business today are intense and unpredictable. Ignoring this uncertainty is tantamount to betting the company on a single outcome of events. In the current business environment this cannot be right for any stakeholder. Managers have to consider various potential scenarios for the future. It is crucially important in order to test important decisions more rigorously, and to be able to react to early indicators of dramatic change. Call it a new more comprehensive form of risk management.

But the greatest reason for training ourselves in thinking about the future is the opportunity it creates for innovation based on anticipated change in the market place, and in this way taking a hand in our own destiny. Scenario planning re-calibrates our entrepreneurial talents, allowing us to re-perceive the world, re-focusing on the green shoots of new trends before others. It does this in an institutional context, creating joint understanding and thereby the ability to move quickly to take advantage of new insights. *For many organizations it will be the key competency in the coming years.*

Professor Kees van der Heijden
Professor of Strategy,
Strathclyde Business School

executive summary

Companies in the developed world face their greatest challenge yet; how to grow profitable revenue and stay alive. For the first time since the middle of this century we have reached a growth plateau in the industrialized world where nil population growth and saturation in consumer goods sectors will radically alter the disposition of the world's largest companies. Only those companies which are the fastest and most innovative in creating new products and services will survive and prosper. At the same time vast untapped markets are emerging in the populous continent of Asia, representing huge opportunities for Western companies together with a number of pitfalls.

Business futurism is a new competence which managers must cultivate in order to be one or two steps ahead of their competitors; to get to the future first but to avoid those damaging mistakes which seemed a good idea at the time.

This book is about how to be a business futurist. Not the variety that belongs in science fiction or cheap sensationalism, but one that is prepared to challenge existing knowledge and preconceptions about the future such as the "this year plus 10 per cent" thinking which still drives most corporate planning in organizations.

This book attempts to look at the world from a multicultural perspective, in the belief that substantive trends transcend borders and are part of a morphic resonance which reverberates across continents; witness Marxism early this century, fascism towards the middle and Thatcherism at the end of it.

The layout of the book has been designed as a handbook for the reader to dip in and out of, very much as some ancient Chinese businessman may have consulted the "I Ching" to plan a new venture. The contents, although far less etherial, are based on a number of interviews conducted around the world with insightful people. This book therefore combines for the first time the technique of being a futurist plus a catalog of current trends which might affect the pace and direction of change.

acknowledgments

I couldn't list all the people who helped formulate the ideas in this book if I tried. However, in addition to the numerous busy people who agreed to be interviewed and all those who shared their innermost thoughts about the future I would like to thank the following:

Liz Morgan, Andy Law, Elaine Sternberger, David Bishop, Genie Turton, Kees van der Heijden, Michael O'Higgins, Andrew Black, Laura Mazur, Anita Hoffmann, Nicky Tan, William Tseng, Jeff Mulgan, Patricia Mann, Robin Bulow, Gill Ringland, Barry Sheerman, Bill Cashmore, Helen Haste, Tim Lang, DeAnne Julius, Hamish Taylor, Hiro Takatsuki, Karena Porcelli, David Birchall, Sheila McKechnie, Anthony Romeo, Eric Salama, Oliver Sparrow, Bob Franke, Bob Worcester, Frank Wetzel, David Griffiths, Terry Squires and Kersten Lanes.

Some special thanks to "John," who gave me three hours of his wisdom on a flight from NY to Miami, to Dave-the-Book, who sparked all this off by giving me an 1897 copy of *The World Next Century*, and to my wife Brenda whose Jungian leanings inspired the Mid-Life Crisis Scenario.

PART ONE

THE BUSINESS FUTURIST – A NEW COMPETENCE

A day in the future

It's 9 a.m. on a Monday morning and you have just dropped your grandchildren off at school. It's time to get back to dealing with the mail you opened two hours earlier. The factory manager in Suzhou, near Shanghai, has been having problems with the latest round of wage negotiations, the distribution franchise in Upper Lombardy wants to terminate the existing contract early, your vice-president of customers wants to get tough with a company selling poor imitations of your product in Dacca and your Research and Development department, outsourced to MIT, are saying that California's new laws would demand 50 percent recyclability of your product and imply fundamental redesign.

It's time to get busy.

Your weekly management conference call is three hours from now at 12.00 GMT and you need to incorporate these issues into an already crowded agenda. Your assistant has also logged on to the network from her home in Prague and you call her up on a window on your workspace. "Good morning, Katia. Nice weekend?" "Great, apart from the sprain. Went skiing with my partner in Austria on Saturday," she replies.

You chose Katia because of her multi-language capability. A language graduate of the University of Prague, she majored in Slavic languages and spent six years with the embassy in Beijing where she picked up a good command of Mandarin. Katia is both interpreter and personal assistant. You found her following a global search on the Net by Persona, the international headhunters for personal assistants.

You ask her to ensure that the entire management team is present for the conference call. Last Monday the VP for production, based in Singapore, was visiting a prospective production facility in Northern Myanmar and couldn't get a stable Sat' connection. The week before, the VP of Finance and Investor Relations, based in New York, had a break-in and thieves took his entire office with them.

Although you have a small central management team, keeping in touch seems to be difficult in this $2bn turnover company. At last month's manage-

ment retreat in the Urals the company shrink, affectionately referred to as Sigmund, had tried to get the group to act as a family. "A family that communicates with each other stays together," had been the concluding message.

While Katia is ensuring that today's meeting will be fully attended and be a productive one, you are opening files on your workspace to remind yourself of the history of the Suzhou negotiations. The original rationale for siting the production facility there was cheap labour rates, and yet now ten years later there are other areas in the region which would offer significant savings. In order to take advantage of the huge 350 million middle class Asian market you have to keep your production costs as low as possible. Is this the time to terminate the Suzhou production contract?

At 10.05 you notice a short message appearing on the screen from the World News Agency that a Malaysian entrepreneur is mounting a hostile bid for your company. If successful, your job, together with those of half your company employees, could be history.

The above beginning to a day in your life 20 years from now, may read like an extract from some science fiction drama but does offer some clues as to what life might be like. What if you were at the forefront of shaping some of these changes in your organization of the future? Could there be future sources of competitive advantage for your company if you were to implement some of the ideas ahead of time?

This book is about finding a mechanism for imagining the future and for creating a rich source of ideas which could help you get to the future first.

■ Prepare to be surprised

Ten years ago I heard the Chief Information Officer of a major corporation address a conference on the electronic office of the coming decade. "The paperless office is about as likely as the paperless toilet," he proclaimed. This sounded most plausible, especially coming from such an informed source. How could we possibly do without the mountains of paper which dominate our lives every day in the office and in the home?

Five years later on a trip to Tokyo I learnt that an entrepreneurial Japanese company had already sold four million toilets which didn't use a scrap of paper. They sprayed warm water where you needed it, hot air to dry you off and left you to go on your way with a hint of fresh roses, something which paper never did for me.

Today many of our working lives are virtually paper-free. Whether in my office, in an hotel room some 7,000 miles away, or in my weekend home, I switch on my e-mail every morning and handle the various requests for help or information. I compose reports and presentations on my lap-top, send them for review on the network, and receive comments back on the same network. Paper has become obsolete in my working life, a liability, tedious and often unread – all this in less than ten years.

Like our CIO, we are invariably caught unaware of the trends affecting our business because we do not spend enough time looking at the future. Our day-to-day lives are spent managing one crisis or another. Most of the senior management running many of our major corporations were last on the front line with customers ten, 20, or more years ago. Talking to them about the forces affecting the enterprise over the next ten or 20 years would be like talking to a bushman about the wonders of space travel.

In fact our belief systems are determined by our early education. Say we grew up in an environment of a stable family unit, went through a male dominated university education, sailed into a career job with a major corporation, and worked largely in unicultural teams. We could be forgiven for thinking that the family unit is indestructible, that men will dominate business thinking forever, that a career job is everybody's aspiration and that multicultural work teams are only in *Star Trek* movies.

We spend most of our mature working lives acting on information and experiences which are out of date. And in today's everchanging market environment our out-of-touchedness is in danger of making the products we sell irrelevant, our organizations redundant and ourselves obsolete.

■ So little time is spent imagining the future

There is an interesting concept put forward by Hamel and Prahalad which they call the 40/30/20 rule. Senior managers were asked three related questions. Number one was: of all available executive time, how much is spent looking outside the immediate confines of the business? That is, looking at external rather than internal issues, not at financial results or key operating ratios, for example, but instead at market implications, or at customer perspectives. Question number two was: of the percentage of the time looking externally, how much of it is genuinely futuristic? Is it spent trying to imagine how things will be in five years, rather than how prices will be affected next year by the change in energy price, for example, or the emergence of a new competitor? Question number three was: of the proportion of time dedicated to gazing into the real future, how much is spent in proper, structured consultation with colleagues with a view to constructing a shared, axiomatic view of the future?

> *Our out-of-touchedness is in danger of making the products we sell irrelevant, our organizations redundant and ourselves obsolete.*

The averaged result from asking these three questions was 40 percent of all time was spent looking externally, of which 30 percent was futuristic, of which 20 percent was in structured consultation. This equates to a mere 2.4 percent of total available time spent on developing a corporate perspective on the future. Clearly, such a low investment will be unlikely to keep us ahead of our competitors and create innovative strategies. As the saying goes, "The future is not what it used to be." But only the innovative companies are going to be in a position to exploit it.

> *Companies need to develop managers with an inbuilt competence to be business futurists.*

Companies need to develop managers with an inbuilt competence to be business futurists. They should take time to look at how the lives of their present and future customers might change and at the products and services they might need. All our lives we have been taught to think backwards. History, the sciences, management thinking, and current affairs are all dominated by the past. The management information we get to run our businesses is based on elapsed activities and we promote people on the assumption that they can repeat past successes.

This book is a manual for the prospective business futurist. We shall be looking at how you can break from tradition and be a forward thinker rather than a backward one. How you can challenge any assumptions about the market based on past events. How you can anticipate change before it actually happens. How you can develop products and services way ahead of your competitors. And, perhaps most importantly, how you can, together with the key stakeholders in your organization, create a shared vision.

> **Be a forward thinker rather than a backward one.**

■ Traditional techniques

Market research

Market research generally is based on the historical beliefs of the customers and their perceptions of the products and services they buy. The newspaper and business articles we read usually refer to historical analysis and comment. By its very nature, market research investigates existing markets, and is excellent in refining existing product propositions. It rarely attempts to probe customers on their views on new product concepts for requirements not yet properly defined.

Benchmarking

Benchmarking has become established as a regular management process in most organizations. By benchmarking we learn how other organizations perform activities in sales, marketing, customer management, and product distribution, to name just a few. We compare ourselves with the best in our industry and discover where we do things better, more or less efficiently. We even benchmark our own products and services against our competitors. All these are excellent operational activities, but none of them help us become a market leader. They do not help us to leapfrog the competition. They would not assist in reinventing our business.

Over the last two years I have led a benchmarking program of over 50 companies in Europe. In the program we examined five key customer management processes, adapted from the Baldrige model of business excellence:

- Understanding customer needs
- Managing customer relationships
- Delivering service through people
- Managing dissatisfaction
- Measuring customer satisfaction.

An overriding conclusion was that innovation in developing the product or service offer was not practiced widely in our group of 50 companies. Analysis revealed that fewer than 5 percent of the organizations had a systematic method for innovating to stay ahead. What they appeared to be doing was watching the competition rather than watching the customer. Most companies put substantial effort into making sure that their offer matched the competition. "Me-too-ism" has clearly been hard at work.

Restructuring

Restructuring has received its fair share of attention in the last ten years. It can mean many different things to different companies, but generally speaking it produced one common result – fewer employees. Between 1990 and 1995 many of the Fortune 500 have literally halved their payroll.

> Many companies have developed an inbuilt competence to cut costs but lost the ability to innovate.

Faced with growing pressure to increase shareholder value, and seeing little or no opportunity for improving revenues, most CEOs felt there was no choice but to use the knife and cut out the corporate fat. But consultants and senior management may not always have been experienced surgeons in such operations, and with the splendid benefit of hindsight some now say that they cut through muscle as well. Many companies have developed an inbuilt competence to cut costs but lost the ability to innovate.

Reengineering

Process reengineering (or transformation) is a much more positive and optimistic activity. While restructuring makes a company smaller, reengineering makes it better. It aims to examine every process in the company's mechanism and then remove unnecessary activities and streamline all those that add value along the supply chain. Now that reengineering is well understood, there is the added benefit that companies are asking their employees to help redesign processes rather than rely on external experts. Once the employees get to grips with the problem and appreciate the objectives, they are more likely to feel a sense of ownership with the issue, and therefore greater commitment.

The reason I have highlighted these activities is that for most companies who have been through the pain barriers involved in undertaking them, the gain has been to catch up with their competitors, rather than getting out in front. But for those companies, now with leaner overheads and meaner operations, and consequent financial stability, there now exists at least the possibility of identifying the road to the future, and setting off down it as fast as possible. The issue now, is how do they decide where the journey starts, and which direction to travel?

> *How do they decide where the journey starts, and which direction to travel?*

If you want to be innovative, don't ask the customer

Over the last 30 years we have seen what is probably best described as three waves of product marketing. In the 1970s, business was largely supply driven, and most companies needed to be efficient order takers. The 1980s was a decade of intense research to ask the customer what he or she wanted, from which companies sought competitiveness. This form of market research has taken on board the height of sophistication in some consumer product areas with a retailer being able to scan transactional level details of each purchase. The third product wave, in which we find ourselves at present, will need to be concept driven. We need to establish what customers might want if it were available or what the customers might want but were too ill-informed to ask.

> *We need to establish what customers might want if it were available or what the customers might want but were too ill-informed to ask.*

Many of the greatest examples of customer concept development have probably stemmed from the belief by an entrepreneur in the changing needs of customers rather than ongoing **product** development.

Mike Bloomberg is today one of the richest men in the United States after launching an information service to the financial services companies at a time

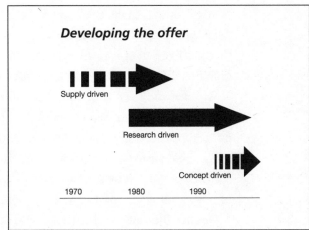

Developing the offer

Supply driven

Research driven

Concept driven

1970   1980   1990

when they were struggling to provide integrated information systems of their own. Although they all had significant technology and software development teams of their own, Bloomberg worked out that a time would come when they would not be able to afford to maintain these teams. There was therefore an opportunity for someone to offer an integrated software package to enable each firm to avoid the enormous development costs over and over again. This "buy not make" policy for software would eventually become accepted best practice.

CNN's success is largely due to Ted Turner having the belief that 24-hour global news television would be watched by millions one day as international business travel increased and new viewing patterns emerged.

Ross Perot, the founding father of Electronic Data Systems (EDS), believed that the outsourcing of systems in companies would be one of the most sought-after services. This, at a time when management gurus were advocating the notion that information technology was one of the key sources of competitive advantage. Today, most companies have outsourced their computer systems, be they accounting, payroll or mission-critical order taking and reservation systems. Outsourcing not only helps control costs but also puts information technology in the hands of expert firms who do nothing else. EDS is today one of the leading providers of systems outsourcing and no company would think of considering outsourcing without calling EDS.

On a smaller scale, the launch of Karaoke TV (KTV) in Asia was initiated over a drinking session by Singapore-based entrepreneur Neil French. The idea came about when someone asked the question "What's the worst thing that could happen to you?" KTV, which appeared to be someone's idea of the "worst" thing, might turn out to be a $2bn business on Asian TV. In most Asian households grandma holds the remote control, and one of the things that she likes most is to hear her family sing. KTV's owners are counting on grandma choosing KTV at prime time rather than another rerun of *Dallas*.

Wunderkind Lars Windhorst had built himself a $200m business before the age of 20 in risk-averse Germany. A high school dropout, he saw a world of opportunity in trading with Asia while the rest of German business kept well away. His business activities range from electronics to film production. Spurned earlier on by the banks and finance institutions, today he is the toast of both politicians and the business community in Germany.

Neither Bloomberg, Turner, nor Perot would have come up with their service offerings by traditional market research. Chief Information Officers in the 1980s were all interested in building their own empires. They boasted bigger and faster mainframes, the latest in software development tools and staff numbers that ran into thousands of people. They wanted more power rather than less. "Buy not make" would not have been of great interest to them. Outsourcing would have diminished or even eliminated their role. Equally not many television viewers at the time would have said that they would watch a 24-hour television news channel.

Neither Bloomberg, Turner, nor Perot would have come up with their service offerings by traditional market research.

But there was already an undercurrent of a number of forces of change which would point to their different businesses succeeding. In Bloomberg's case it was the escalating cost of information systems that was becoming burdensome with repeated mega overruns in project cost and timescales; software took so long to develop that it was redundant by the time the programs had been tested successfully. For Perot, the forces of change regarding the focus on core business activities

Imagine if you could identify the forces of change in your business.

were already building momentum, and for Turner fast-moving events such as the 1987 Wall Street shock and the Gulf War began to make 24-hour news a necessity for many.

Imagine if you could identify the forces of change in your business and begin to reformulate your own product or service proposition to shape the future in your own markets.

The forces of change are complex

Customers exist at every level in the supply chain, and long before the product or service reaches the final end-user, there may have been several sellers and several buyers. In a typical business-to-business customer/supplier relationship, the three categories of customer are:

- The economic buyer
- The decision maker
- The influencer or user.

Change may affect each one differently, and our future proposition must reflect the needs of each one independently and together as a whole.

The economic buyer's motivation in the purchasing decision may be to keep within the budget constraints for a group of purchases. This buyer will be asking questions such as "Will I make my budget?" and "Is this the best deal around?" The decision maker may want to make the correct decision with regard to risk and personal reputation. The influencer or user may be motivated primarily by other users of the product. Issues such as: "Do any of our competitors use this product?" or "Can I get a reference from somebody else?" would be addressed by this type of buyer.

Now let's assume that changes in the way companies organize themselves in the future might de-emphasize boundaries between suppliers, buyers, and end user customers. The emergence of the virtual organization leads to thinking about partnerships with a few suppliers. GM, GE, and Ford, to name but three, have reduced their supplier count by orders of magnitude. Long-term relationships and incentivized payments for quality and performance will become the order of the day.

Because future customer values will inevitably change to reflect these changes, we will see motivations change to buyers taking a far more longer-sighted view. The economic buyer will be considering the decision more in terms of lifetime value. The decision maker will be thinking more about the long-term partnership into which the company is entering. The influencer/end user will be trying to imagine how the relationship might stand up when things start going wrong. In each case the buyers will be thinking less of themselves and more of the long-term implications to the company of the relationship.

Are your management evaluating how customer values are changing and seeking to keep pace?

By reading this far, I suggest you should now be asking yourself if your company is thinking more about the future than the past, or even the present. Are your management evaluating how customer values are changing and seeking to keep pace? Ask youself the following questions:

1. *Does your management team take time out at least once a year to look at the future needs of customers for a forward duration which is at least greater than the standard payback period of an investment in your organization?*

2. *Does your search for the future extend to the forces affecting all "customers" or stakeholders in your supply chain?*

3. *Is your review wider than industy data or forecasts and incorporating views of outsiders who may affect or influence the needs of your customers?*

4. *Is your business based on more than one view or set of outcomes for the future?*

5. *Does your management team have a shared vision of the future?*

If the answers were "no" to most of the above questions then I would suggest that you are in an organization which exists for the present and may be trading on the historical loyalties of your customers and the image you have in the marketplace. If you are in an increasingly competitive market, then you are vulnerable and your future existence is in question. If I were a shareholder in your business, I'd be calling my broker with a strong "sell" order.

> *Once you have got through to the end, come back and ask yourself these questions again.*

The following pages in this book will attempt to show you how you might be able to answer "yes" to the above questions. Once you have got through to the end, come back and ask yourself these questions again. It is my sincere hope that you might be convinced to take on board some of the processes described in the coming chapters.

PART TWO

THE VECTORS OF CHANGE

This part deals with the vectors of change which will determine the customers of the future. It is probably impossible to include all that will affect the course of the future. These are the factors which a range of people have identified as relevant to the next 20 years, people who I believe are insightful thinkers about the changes going on in the world today. They come from a variety of backgrounds: politicians, educators, marketeers, journalists, technologists, strategists, economists, and social scientists, to name but a few. Also included are the sentiments expressed in some of my most read and respected publications, over the eighteen month period I researched the contents of this book.

I have used the term "vectors of change" because vector implies not only speed but also direction. In looking at the future we are interested both in the speed with which change is likely to occur but also which direction events might take. Globalization, for example, might take two divergent routes: one of them might involve the progressive lifting of trade barriers whilst the other might take the form of increasing resistance in the developed world emanating from concern about the constant export of jobs.

The brainstorming is by its nature a selection of random thoughts which we have reproduced to capture the thinking that evolves in a scenario development. Although you might find some of the logic difficult to follow there are a number of gems of ideas embedded in the vox pop dialog.

How you should use this part of the book

The vectors described in this chapter are wide ranging and it is impossible to prioritize any of them in order of impact or importance to any individual. They all have a different significance to each one of you. Many who work in companies which are internationalizing their businesses will no doubt feel that the "Shrinking World" is perhaps the most pertinent to their future. Yet others developing products and services to the consumers may be interested in "The Family" and the future of "Work." Those of you who are involved in retailing and may need to answer the difficult question of how to enhance your brand would be interested primarily in the attitudes of "post-consumerism."

The brainstorming group: (from left to right) Kees van der Heijden, Andrew Black, Bill Cashmore, Laura Mazur, Michael O'Higgins, Anita Hoffmann, Glen Peters, Barry Sheerman, Gill Ringland.

My intention in creating this part of the book was to provide a checklist of the typical vectors of change to help you with developing scenarios for change in your organizations. It is by no means an exhaustive list and some of the information may be known to the "wired" reader. But I hope it is a start to your research into the vectors which most affect you.

Here is a summary of the vectors of change and their importance to the executive who wants to get to the future first.

The shrinking world

Communications, air travel, falling barriers to trade and convergence of taste and preference have been contributing to the development of one open world. There are however countervailing forces against globalization in both the developed and developing world. The company in the midst of globalizing its brands and seeking to grow new markets abroad will need to be aware of the opportunities being created in the world and how to anticipate the trouble spots.

Some have referred to this vector in more radical terms as the "end" of the nation state. Whereas many of the people I have interviewed prefer to take this more severe view, the consensus seems to be that the nation state is changing from one of centralized government to a more decentralized form. This change takes place with a background of disillusionment with government and its ability to counter consider-

The decline of nation state

ably stronger international market forces. The transfer of governmental powers to states, counties and communities, both local and global (e.g. Greenpeace) is of significance to organizations who sell services to government institutions or those that might be affected by this fragmentation of power.

At the turn of the century 4 percent of the US population was over 65, but in 20 years' time that figure will have risen to 25 percent. The developed world is ageing and governments cannot afford to maintain welfare programs at the same level over the next decade. As boomers retreat to the stock market, as their major insurance against future loss of earnings, they have created one of the longest running bull

The end of state dependency – the privatization

markets. The privatization of welfare represents a major opportunity for all those service organizations which provide care, pensions and a secure future for the individual before and after retirement. Their scenario plans must establish a vision of how the private sector will rise to this challenge.

The transformation of work

The job, product of the industrial revolution, may be completely transformed into a more temporary arrangement between employee and employer. We expect to see individuals having to take more responsibility for their own careers, more self-employment and a substantial rise in telecommuting. Add greater job insecurity and a drift to a low wage world and suddenly anyone in business today, planning their personal future, will find this vector to be of the utmost interest to them.

The haves and have-nots

The world and many societies within it have always been separated on economic grounds. The last decade has seen a far greater separation between the rich and poor countries and between the haves and have-nots within the rich countries. If this gap is left to widen we could be heading towards a deeply divided world, the inevitable result of which would be either regional or global conflict. The great steps made in encouraging world trade and ending the 50-year cold war could be reversed. Businesses affected by this crude segmentation should set signposts in its future plans to track the development of the widening gap and the accompanying breakdown of social order. Companies should also be aware of the contribution that they can make to arresting or reversing this trend.

Resourcing the world

Whilst an energy shortfall worried forecasters 20 years ago, today they are concerned about the availability of an even more basic commodity; food and water. As countries like China rise in economic power they will make huge demands on the world's food supplies. Worldwide trade in basic resources will be of interest to consumer product companies and suppliers of raw materials.

This is the name given to the consumer group that has everything. With demand for consumer durables near saturation point in the developed world and with customers of the newly industralized world in the East wanting the most up-to-date products available in the West, companies are facing highly demanding consumers. These consumers reject traditional marketing and want to be dealt with as individuals

Post-consumerism

to whom brand loyalty is a secondary consideration. Retailers, direct marketeers and all businesses concerned with selling to the end-consumer will need to adopt appropriate responses to these trends.

The family is changing out of all recognition. A third of children in the US today are born out of wedlock and divorce has been rising throughout the world. We can see two outcomes; the nuclear family changes to a more loosely coupled unit or society acts to reverse this trend. Either option has implications for organizations such as house builders companies and all those involved in the provision of products and ser-

The end of patriarchy

vices where choice and selection may be determined by the structure of the family.

Women the world over have been rising in their importance in influencing buying behavior and political change. They are obtaining higher educational qualifications than men and are voting more in opposition to men for the preservation of welfare. Women's needs as consumers have been largely neglected by companies and their rise in power and influence will be ignored to the detriment of marketeers.

The ascent of women

Commoditizing communications technology

According to futurists such as Alvin and Heidi Toffler we have entered a new age, one of information and knowledge. Its "brains" will drive the economies of the future rather than "brute force" which fuelled the industrial revolution. The speed with which countries rise to the challenge of the information age will be dependent on how much they are prepared to invest in the infrastructure and training needed to compete. Companies that can make effective use of these new channels of distribution to customers will open up global markets for a fraction of the investment needed for the bygone age of tangible products. The use of the Internet and its associated technologies represents the most significant opportunity for companies who wish to shape the future in these emerging areas of selling knowledge and information.

The fragile earth

Our fragile earth is beginning to show significant signs of the effects of "human activity" in the form of extreme weather conditions and the depletion of the ozone layer causing extensive areas of the world where the sun's rays are harmful to people. Consumers the world over are concerned about the effects of the changing environment on our future world. Nowhere is this concern more pronounced than with young people; the consumers of tomorrow. Any company whose processes may have a harmful impact on the environment will be increasingly censored by pressure groups which will be able to do untold damage by exercising the customer's ultimate weapon, the boycott.

Competition for education

The role of education in the developed world will be emphasized more than in recent times with people having to take on more individual responsibility for life-long learning. The state will play a diminished funding role as education becomes more globalized and the world's leading institutions are predominated by students who attend courses remotely from around the world.

Educationalizing products will be seen to be a source of differentiating the most mundane items we buy, as learning is sought after by everyone as a route to success. Any organization involved in education, or in seeking to offer learning as an extension of their existing services, must thoroughly explore the future of this vector.

The vectors of change – political forces

The shrinking world

The shrinking world is our first vector in this book and it will be a major consideration when developing scenarios where the customer is affected by the globalization of business. Advances in communications technology, the falling cost of air travel and the opening up of trade will expose the customer to a profusion of choice. If we are to begin to answer questions as to the future of say "The English Pub" then we must understand the influences of the shrinking world on people who visit pubs in England and those who might want to visit one elsewhere in the world. In this chapter we deal with some of the trends which have already begun. If we want to assess the implications for global branding then we need to be aware of the implications of satellite television on the mass consumer markets emerging in Asia.

Highlights

- *The internationalization of business*
- *Uncertainty in the Japanese equity markets*
- *The emergence of common tastes*
- *The snacking culture*
- *Regionalism*
- *The counter forces of globalization*

■ Internationalization of business

Over the last ten years the world has witnessed a growing internationalization of its businesses. The trend referred to as globalization relies on the economies of scale for seeking out larger markets. The wider the global company's portfolio the more it is insulated from a downturn in one region. While Europe has been in recession in the early 1990s, Asia has been booming. This trend towards foreign investment by companies will continue to increase with every Fortune 500 company having some ambition to being a global player.

Western companies, and in particular those offering consumer products, have enjoyed improved profitability ahead of their competitors who may have elected to focus more on home markets in the developed world. Guinness, the company famous for its distinctive beer and also associated with other brands such as Bell's Scotch whisky and Gordon's gin, is one such example. Its international markets, influenced heavily by the fast-growing Asian sector, produced margins twice that of its domestic market in Europe. Guinness, with its international operations at nearly 45 percent of its total business, gave it a lead against its competitors Grand Metropolitan and Allied Domecq, who are more dependent on European markets where less brand-conscious consumers are more reluctant to accept price increases.

A number of banks have been trying to internationalize their operations in what has traditionally been a business which has been confined to national boundaries. Citicorp and the Hong Kong Shanghai Banking Corporation have been spreading their retail banking operations around the world, whilst several of the large US and European banks have, through mergers and acquisitions, sought to compete for the world's investment banking business.

Some banks such as J P Morgan and Shearson Lehman have begun to create international niches in developing services for specific groups of customers, who have been uncomfortable with traditional banks. Followers of Islam reject the charging of interest for loans.

The US financial firms dominate the world market and neither the European nor Japanese banks are likely to alter this position for some time. The *Wall Street Journal* refered to this in a lead article as the "Americanization of finance." Names like Goldman, Sachs & Co., J P Morgan, and Merrill Lynch & Co. dominate privatizations, mergers, takeovers, and global underwriting activities for both US and European clients. Industry watchers argue that the days when "close relationships" between client and banker determined the choice of financial adviser are gone. The job usually goes to the firm with the most innovative financial package to meet client needs.

> *75 percent of managers felt that globalization was their greatest issue of interest.*

The American Management Association survey of its members in 1995 showed that over 75 percent of managers felt that globalization was their greatest issue of interest. Although many US companies have been multinational since the 1960s, George Yip, professor of strategy at Anderson School of Management in LA, believes that they have not been global. Being global, he defines, is taking advantage of global markets and their economies of scale, and being culturally representative of the markets in which the companies operate.

Thus merely having a plant or selling operation in a country would not classify a company as being global. Imposing the dominant parent culture, be it Japanese or American, would not qualify a company as being global. The

> **The transition from being multinational to global will be necessary if companies are to command the respect of citizens in the new world markets they will serve.**

transition from being multinational to global will be necessary if companies are to command the respect of citizens in the new world markets they will serve. These companies will have to apply the same standards of safety, reliability, and product quality on a global basis rather than selectively as they may previously have done. In other words a universal code of business ethics will become necessary to survive globalization.

Many multinational companies are stepping up their efforts to hire local managers for overseas positions. Traditionally US companies have expatriated their own managers for foreign postings but rising costs and the need to internationalise their personnel policies have given rise to hiring native-born employees. As a result over the last ten years the number of personnel employed overseas by the top 250 US companies has increased by a quarter of a million. A 1996 survey by Cushman and Wakefield showed that Asia was the largest region for expanding offshore operations at 44% with Europe and South America coming in at 23% and 14% respectively.

Expansion has also been travelling from East to West. Ispat International Limited is a British based steel company, one of the ten largest in the world and owned by India's leading family dynasty. It has acquired operations in Germany, Ireland, Mexico and is currently the biggest investor in the former Soviet Union. Its $1bn investment in Kazakhstan's Karmet steel plant makes it a global industry player and a frightening competitor.

■ Japanese equity markets

The collapse of the Japanese equity markets in the early 1990s may signal a change in the way companies have been run in that country. For the last few decades, investors have enjoyed substantial capital gains with meagre earnings from dividends. Without the capital gain enjoyed in previous years, shareholders and, in particular, institutional investors who act on behalf of the large pension funds will put pressure on Japanese companies to run their companies along Anglo-Saxon lines.

Ron Dore of the London School of Economics argues that employee-sovereignity will give way to shareholder-sovereignity for Japanese companies as the internationalization of capital markets will create competition for Japanese investors' capital. Western markets, where they may be assured at least of earnings from dividends if not capital gain, may benefit following a period of yen/dollar stability.

■ Common tastes

For many years marketeers have sought the holy grail of homogenous global brands where companies can take economies of scale in marketing and manufacturing costs. Local and national preferences have so far dogged the global marketeer. Despite the Japanese love of sushi, the Germans clinging to the wurst and the French to their own wines, there is evidence of a growing acceptance of, and in some cases yearning for, cross-cultural tastes.

In recent years this has been demonstrated by McDonald's, the icon of the hamburger, Perrier, the company that made water fashionable worldwide, and Body Shop, the outlet for the environmentally conscious consumer. Every year new brands emerge, trying to cross the barriers of national and cultural preferences.

No country has been more successful in co-packaging its own culture together with its brands than the United States. Coca-Cola, McDonald's, Disney, Hollywood, and Levi's have been promoted on the back of a country that has espoused freedom of the individual, youth, innovation, and wealth. Packaging Americana has taught other countries that the world can be viewed as one market and can enhance the profitability of companies back home.

McDonald's has 20 percent of the US$90 billion per annum hamburger market, which has made it a household name synonymous with the Stars And Stripes, motherhood, and apple pie. Recently, megabrands have begun to co-promote products. When Disney released the animation feature *Pocahontas*, McDonald's promoted the film in its outlets and offered a special Pocahontas hamburger for the duration of the film's general release.

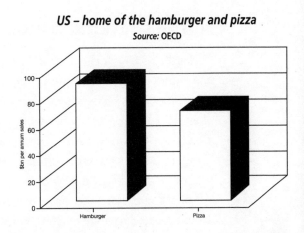

US – home of the hamburger and pizza
Source: OECD

Result: every kid that saw the film wanted to go to McDonald's to sample its special hamburgers and every kid that went to McDonald's pestered his or her parents to go and see the film to find out what all the fuss was about.

The consumption of pizza, once exclusively Italian, is one of the newer additions to a worldwide market. Germans apparently eat 12 times more pizza than Italians, and although each culture would undoubtedly have its own toppings and flavors, the pizza is now an international dish.

> **Sport too has become a great unifier of national tastes.**

Growing awareness about health is also giving rise to brands associated with health consciousness, and breakfast cereals are one example where the cornflake and bowl of muesli have taken over from the sausage, the egg, and other things which heart attacks are made of.

Sport too has become a great unifier of national tastes. Spurred on mainly by satellite TV, soccer, tennis, car racing, and athletics, brands like Nike and Reebok have taken advantage of promoting their products using the superstars which millions watch on their screens worldwide.

There is evidence that this trend will continue. But we are still some way from the Levitian idea of global brands for all. The theme for the next decade seems to be macro brands with a micro overlay for local preferences. Coca-Cola sells a sweeter version of its drink in the north of Japan to suit regional preferences, and McDonald's serves a no-beef hamburger in Delhi because Indians believe the cow is sacred. Perhaps a Manhattan consumer sums it all up by the comment, "I've tasted pizzas everywhere in the world but nowhere do they make pizza as good as they do in New York."

> **macro brands with a micro overlay for local preferences.**

■ The snacking culture

When British Airways launched its 1995 rebranding campaign, it redesigned mealtimes on board aircraft. Rather than cabin crew serving meals at set times to business-class passengers, they offered travelers the opportunity to help themselves from a snack bar whenever they liked. Hamish Taylor, Managing Director of Brands, said, "Our research has shown that people are eating smaller amounts but more often." The trials with customers have been a great success, confirming this trend.

Snacks and fast food have played well to the lifestyles we lead and the United States has done much to perpetuate the snacking culture. This has spilt over into "mini-treat occasions" and provided the opportunity for a number of retail concepts to spring up where the individual seeks a break during the every-day course of events.

Seattle-based Starbucks, the coffee shop chain with 650 outlets throughout the US, is such an example, with customers spending around $4 per head for unusual concoctions of coffee such as moccachino, frappuchino, a low-fat iced coffee, and mazagran, a lightly carbonated version. The outlets, with their cool decor and fashionable image, bring the average cus-tomer back to Starbucks around four times a week. Howard Schultz, Starbucks' founder, puts the con-cept's success down to the fact that his shops are offer-ing the option of a "third place" between the office and home. The ability to create a luxury proposition around coffee, which has been highly commoditized by the endlesss cups of coffee consumed in the office and at home, must play to a growing need.

Global executives are spending more time on airplanes than in their offices or homes.

Similar successes have also been recorded by UK-based Costa Bros whose range of 30 gourmet coffee shops, mainly at railway stations, was recently acquired by Whitbread.

■ World cities

Rosabeth Moss Kanter in her book *World Class* believes that the future division in society will be between locals and cosmopolitans rather than

PROFILE OF A COSMOPOLITAN:
- Geneva-based but spends 234 days per annum away
- Carries a mobile office on his pc
- Always in touch using two GSN phones to connect to the office network anywhere in the world
  David Arkless-VP Manpower

the traditional capital versus labor. However, she makes a strong case for globalization being a powerful way to regenerate cities of the world, and her three examples of Boston, Miami and Spartanburg, South Carolina, are cited as examples. Her solution is that cities have to be world class in either thinking, manufacturing, or trading to attract companies.

Division in society will be between locals and cosmopolitans.

Cities like London and New York have become world cities where the global elite are more likely to congregate. In these cities you can probably eat any food in the world, and find someone who speaks a speci-fic language or dialect, or has an obscure technical qualification or expertise.

When the European Bank set up its offices in London, it found that it could staff most of its language and technical skills requirements from within the city, rather than having to resort to expatriate personnel. London has become world class, in Ms Kantor's terms, as a major financial center and contributes increasingly to Britain's GDP. Despite short-term setbacks in the liberalization of its Stock Exchange, the long-term prospects for the City as a key financial centre look promising.

Kuala Lumpur, the Malaysian capital, will soon have the world's two tallest office towers, and work is also under way to build a new megacity to rival Tokyo and Yokohama. Called Putrajaya, it will be the commercial capital of the country by 2008. With cars being discouraged, the infrastructure of this "garden city" will rival any Western city, with tramways and light transit railways.

Singapore is cloning itself by creating satellite cities in other Asian countries such as China and India. Suzhou, the 70 sq km Chinese township west of Shanghai, will have $20 billion invested in it to create a gateway for Singapore to China. Already several Western companies are being attracted by the idea of setting up their Chinese operations in Suzhou because of the "disciplined and ordered" approach of the Singaporeans. By negotiating long-term leases Singapore intends to create other cities modeled on its own image and create a business climate for it to build a gateway into the rest of Asia. Singapore itself intends to move out all heavy, labor-intensive manufacturing to the satellites, to take advantage of the low labor rates in these countries.

■ Regionalism

While companies have been seeking to internationalize their businesses, countries have been getting together to form regional trading blocks. The World Trade Organization estimates that over 100 trade organizations currently exist. One of the concerns of the WTO is that powerful groupings will impose unequal terms on weaker countries to their disadvantage.

> *The World Trade Organization estimates that over 100 trade organizations currently exist.*

The US and the EU are by far the most advanced trading blocks according to John Robinson, a partner responsible for cross-border trading at Price Waterhouse. Trade between US and Canada within the NAFTA region accounts for $1 billion per day between the two countries and contributes to keeping four million jobs, whilst trade between the US and the entire EU accounts for less than $100 billion per annum. Member countries in the EU have little autonomy in creating bi-lateral trading agreements and the entire federation is governed by a single set of trading rules. ASEAN, the SE Asian federation, is about five to ten years behind in its ability to create a single trading entity like the EU. China, although not currently a member of the World Trade Organization, could take its place as one of the world's largest trading entities early next century.

Regionalism would affect the developed world most. In a wider Europe, for example, where the population is expected to remain static at half a billion, growth will be significantly compromised without access to the growing markets in the emerging economies of the world.

■ Globalization – counter forces

Despite the strong push for globalizing businesses and the marketing of global brands, there will be a backlash by nationalist sentiment against this trend. India's Hindu nationalist party wants to slow the influence of multinations, and demonstrators have smashed Pepsi bottles and set fire to Kentucky Fried Chicken restaurants as a protest against Western consumer projects. But the country has, for the last 50 years, been used to socialist, anti-colonialist thinking and many observers argue that this backlash is similar to the campaigns organized against the multinationals in Europe in the late 1960s and 1970s. Indian states are likely to begin competing for foreign investment in future, with the more progressive ones courting foreign input aggressively. A consortium which included Siemens and Powergen recently signed a $270m sixteen-year loan package to help finance a power station in Gujarat. Unlike the Enron deal, the Western consortium in this instance chose to link up with an Indian partner.

> *There will be a backlash by nationalist sentiment against this trend.*

Critics of globalization are also to be heard of in the West. Sociologists like Amitai Etzioni argue that globalization is destroying jobs and communities. A worldwide head of production can shut down a plant in, say, Detroit and move it to Delhi without knowing or feeling the social impact of the decision on the communities involved. Well-known capitalists like Sir James Goldsmith and Ross Perot believe that the export of jobs to the third world is orchestrated by an international elite of managers who, every day, distance themselves further from the local communities in which they live. The 1996 US presidential campaign featured Pat

> *Globalization is destroying jobs and communities.*

Buchanan, the republican candidate, expressing highly conservative views from the closing of America's borders to the export of jobs and bringing back memories of the "Come home America" calls not heard since the 1930s.

Brainstorming the consequences

Technologist: Even though there are 500 million potential customers in a wider Europe, barriers would be unhealthy since innovation comes from a global wash of ideas across borders.

Strategist: What is the optimal size of unit for production and consumption? In the US there are a lot of regional brands, regional retailers, etc. Could the same be true in Europe? Can you stay local/regional in the face of international competition? Shell came to the conclusion that there were real economies of scale by transitioning from country units to, say, a European entity. Although we could see a significant improvement of productivity by regionalizing our business, economies of scale did not operate in the same way in a wider theater. In other words the economies of scale did not extend to full globalization.

> **Innovation comes from a global wash of ideas across borders.**

Author: But industries like software and entertainment are already becoming global. Transport is almost free because it is an electronic medium. At the other end of the spectrum where transport is a big factor, such as in gasoline distribution, economies of scale cease to operate the further you get from your sources of production. Health, retailing, etc. may also be subject to diseconomies of scale because of national rules or restrictions, or indeed consumer preference. IKEA was perhaps the first global retailer I can recall. Maybe furniture and household goods do not suffer the same problems.

Economist: But aren't the growth rates of what are global companies comparatively low? And most of these are doing significant downsizing.

Strategist: The truly global company is the one that has worked out the optimal distribution and production pattern.

Sociologist: In the 1980s the Japanese coming to the UK were very centralized, bringing components in from Japan, and it was very profitable because Japan had such an undervalued exchange rate. Ten years later, the yen goes through the roof and the centralized system becomes a liability. The problem now is how do the Japanese go on making their global brands in an environment that isn't Japanese and with a home market priced out of existence? It should make one cautious about creating certain structures.

Author: But that is also an argument for going global – you can balance levels of exposure in different markets, a downturn in one may be compensated by an upturn in another. My hunch is that customers will be offered products which may be produced regionally but are conceived or designed centrally. We already see this with, say, Japanese cars which are produced locally in Europe or North America but are designed centrally in Japan for the world markets.

The vectors of change – political forces

The decline of the nation state

If your customer groupings are significantly affected by governmental policy then this vector will play a major part in your scenarios. If you are a defense contractor, say, then the ability of government to radically alter defense expenditure will be of considerable interest to you. We have titled this vector The Decline of The Nation State because from our research and interviews there was general agreement that nations in future would be far less able to act on their own. We see below why many countries are becoming disenfranchized.

Highlights

- *Markets vs nations*
- *Disillusionment with politicians*
- *The decline of the United Nations*
- *Defense*
- *China's political stalemate*

> "There is no such thing as countries; only land, rivers, hills and fields"
>
> *David Niven*

Popular themes

Disillusionment with politicians and their ability to effect change. The decline of parliaments. The downgrading of official world bodies. The rise of communitarianism. The sociopolitical activists, e.g. Greenpeace, NRA. Virtual communities. Terrorism on a megascale. The end of the nation state. The creation of 100 new countries. The Orwellian state. The fragility of Asian politics. The Asian arms race. The democratization of South-East Asia.

■ Markets vs nation states

Investment flows and inflows between countries have risen dramatically over the last ten years as barriers to trading have been lowered. As a result the power of governments to tax, borrow, or increase the money supply is being determined more by how international markets view a particular policy than the need to pursue a particular ideology.

Although the EU has made some progress in achieving standardization, worldwide there is little evidence that countries are begining to harmonize their economic policies to evolve a common standard acceptable to the world's financial markets. There are wide differences in the public spending by government in, say, Sweden at 70 percent and Singapore at under 20 percent. Taxation policies also differ widely from country to country, as does the ability to control inflation and interest rates. However, the shrinking world could give rise to fewer disparities between taxation regimes in one country versus another. Countries like Denmark, for example, whose tax and social security contributions add up to 51 percent of a person's income, will have to make choices between the extent to which it is prepared to support welfare programs and how far it is prepared to risk the relocation of businesses in lower cost and lower taxation regimes.

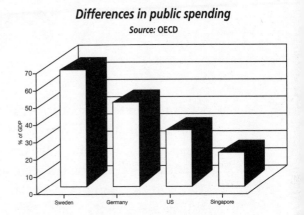

Differences in public spending
Source: OECD

So far, however, few European countries have actually lowered their public spending and cut taxation. France in 1995 took the option to increase taxation in order to close the budget deficit to meet the 3 percent target set by the European Union. Most analysts see this as having a negative effect. The biggest casualty could be growth, which inevitably slows when taxes are increased. Many

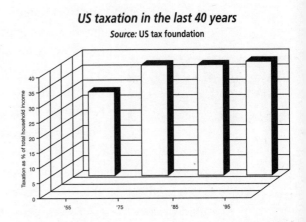

US taxation in the last 40 years
Source: US tax foundation

Taxation and unemployment

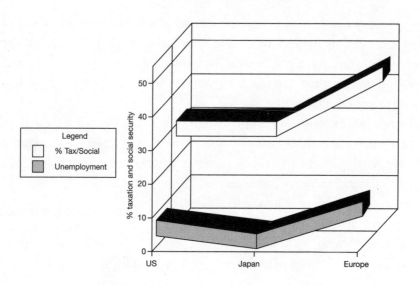

point to Hong Kong, soon to become part of the People's Republic of China, as an example where low taxation at 15 percent has produced a 3 percent unemployment rate, one of the lowest in the world.

United States taxation has been on the way up since 1955 from around 27 percent to 38 percent in 1995. The "cut taxes" lobby led by Newt Gingrich could be seen as a reaction to reverse this trend.

■ Disillusionment with politicians

In Britain a 1994 poll showed that less than 20 percent of voters believed that politicians could effect change. The figure in 1950 was over 70 percent. In most of the democratic world politicians are aware of the international forces of trade and the global financial markets, and believe that they are losing the freedom to introduce radicalism into their policies that they once enjoyed. This has been reflected in the willingness of citizens to participate in the political process. Fewer people are voting and engaging in political activism.

Fewer people are voting and engaging in political activism.

The changes in tax rate for corporations or high net worth individuals usually results in the expatriation of earnings to some foreign low tax regime. The changes in interest rates are almost immediately reflected in the strength or weakness of the national currency, and markets wait in a round-the-clock vigil for those vulnerable economies to make a move.

Similarly exchange rates are determined not by government policy but by the market's view of the economic strength of a country.

Contrast this view with the fact that in most developed economies governments are responsible for a substantial slice of a country's income and there is evidence that they are controlling more of this income rather than less of it. *The Economist* in a well argued

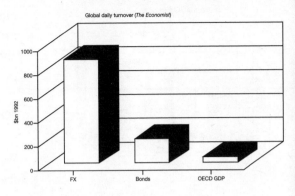

Markets dwarf nations' GDP

Global daily turnover (*The Economist*)

leader said that "The barriers (to international trade) that politicians have lowered can be raised again. Protectionists, such as Perot and Goldsmith, who demand the trend of global integration be reversed, are frightening precisely

because, given the will, governments could do it. Call it their sovereign right."

Two other countervailing forces in the decline of the nation state are the inability of world bodies like the United Nations to intervene effectively in global conflict and national control over defense expenditure.

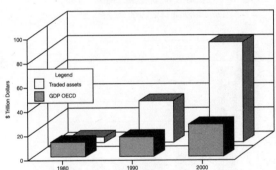

Capital markets get on top

Source: McKinsey

■ The decline of the United Nations

The inability of the United Nations to resolve a number of conflicts from Somalia to Bosnia has led to a growing disillusionment with this body in a post-Cold War era. One of the institution's biggest problem is its huge $4 billion unpaid debt, with the largest sum owed by the US.

The pax-Americana status attained by the US after the collapse of the Soviet Union has led increasingly to the former dominating world foreign policy. The 18 month ceasefire in Northern Ireland, the cessation of hostilities in Bosnia and the Middle East peace agreements can be largely attributed to the involvement of the US in varying degrees. Professor Paul Roger of the University of Bradford Peace Studies faculty argues that too much power and

% Voting and politically active (UK)
Source: MORI/Socioconsult

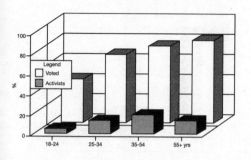

influence residing with the US and its Northern European allies sums the risk of further deepening the split between rich and poor countries.

■ Defense

Overall defense spending in the post-Cold War era has declined. However, spending in the Pacific Rim and the Middle East continues to increase. The Japanese defense ministry puts its own increase down to the need to raise expenditure from a very low base. The current level of expenditure puts the US way ahead of other countries, giving it the military strength to intervene in any area of conflict which threatens its position in any way. However US defense contractors have seen pressure to reduce procurement expenditure and a substantive consolidation of companies in this sector will continue.

Defense expenditure comparisons – 1995
Source: Institute of Strategic Studies

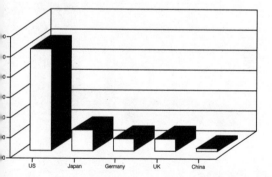

■ China's political stalemate

In his book *Governing China* Kenneth Lieberthal, one of America's most respected China experts, argues that China has not evolved a stable political system to keep in check its most powerful leaders. Although the system is less dictatorial than most Westerners believe, economic reform has substantially weakened the formal and informal systems. Governing China is now a continual sequence of negotiations between local, provincial, and national leaders, which Lieberthal describes as "fragmented authoritarianism." There is therefore little agreement on how to proceed with economic reform. Several commentators point to a potential annexation of Taiwan, the death of Deng and the 1997 takeover of Hong Kong as key events to watch.

Brainstorming the consequences

Do states still have a lot of power? They still control on average more than half of the GDP.

Politician: We have witnessed a revolution in the end of the experiments in command economies – not just the Soviet model. Also, what is significant is that it is the end of the isolated economy. You can choose to be a Cuba, but in a democracy that isn't an option. We are part of a global economy and global politics, with regional dimensions such as the European Union making that even more immediate. Anything we do at the country level is sensitive to changing investment decisions elsewhere by multinational companies and other governments.

> *We have witnessed a revolution in the end of the experiments in command economies.*

Sociologist: The state-government has grown to become a big service provider. But any company of this size that has matured to this stage after 40–60 years would have gone bust or have to reinvent itself quite radically. We are still facing the challenge of changing on a more regular and dynamic basis. How do you build dynamism into state institutions?

> *The state-government has grown to become a big service provider.*

Technologist: Should politicians do it? Do they want to run the state apparatus? Shouldn't people do that by vote? Soon technology will allow them to do that. It gets back to people being disconnected from government, not voting. There is apathy, especially in the US. What they are doing is picking up issue politics – Greens, etc. Possibly this is down to the idea of instant gratification – people get angry and want to do something instantly.

Politician: We have got used to consumerist attitudes in other parts of life. People want to bring in consumerist thinking, making a stand on areas like local libraries, export of live animals, and so on. People are looking for a different way. Politicians recognize that there are much greater limits on activities. Politics is not really about who gets what where, when, and how, but recognizing the limitations around each of those. That is the new approach. People understand that they need to make their country competitive to create wealth.

> *People want to bring in consumerist thinking, making a stand on areas like local libraries, export of live animals, and so on.*

Economist: There are a number of issues always confronting societies where either "might is right" – whoever has the deepest pocket, the ability to bribe – will probably end up having a disproportionate influence, or a framework is accepted which has to have checks and balances built in. So though the role of the state may be being pushed

> *So though the role of the state may be being pushed back, the state keeps getting hauled into the arena at regular intervals to adjudicate and act as an umpire between the various groups.*

back, the state keeps getting hauled into the arena at regular intervals to adjudicate and act as an umpire between the various groups. The umpiring role needs to be seen rather differently. The whole way the government machine is set up needs to be examined. It is supposed to take a long-term view and not be persuaded by the latest "bribe," but there is a complex issue about how far it should be a stabilizer and how far it should react quickly to requests, and how far it should avoid being the plaything of interest groups.

Technologist: Nigel Lawson, an ex-UK Chancellor, said how relaxing he found going into business after politics, with its quarterly audits. In government people are panicking about things on a day-to-day basis. Is this the way it should behave?

> *If people turn against politics, do they turn to private markets/means to do things?*

Sociologist: Is it politics and markets, or politics against markets? What happens if politics itself becomes a competing market? If people turn against politics, do they turn to private markets/means to do things?

Technologist: Communications and the role of the media are central here. And new technology can be used to create a single face of government. Factors like giving citizens access with the Internet and the resulting two-way communication will have an impact, as with the electronic elections favored by people like Ross Perot.

> *Is the case for representative democracy slipping by default?*

Economist: Do we need representative democracy any more? Should regular referenda be carried out? Is the case for representative democracy slipping by default?

Author: Why couldn't we have a chief executive elected to run parts of government such as infrastructure, roads, railways, education, etc? Like mayors and cities? The CEOs would implement policy and a very small elected group of politicians would be responsible for developing policy based on their electoral mandate.

Economist: You could end up with a classic monopolist who tends to reduce the supply of service that you have to have. He can raise the revenue to pay for it with taxes, but has no particular incentive to make sure people get it. That distribution problem is a reason for governments.

Actor: Don't forget the effect of the media on attitudes, it can be powerful: the Berlin Wall came down because the media made it obsolete.

Author: Will China stay unified or will it break-up like the Soviet Union? We need to be aware of the psychology of countries – China has thousands of years of history as a powerful empire run by a strong central figure. The 18th-century explorers discovered this when they tried to trade with the then emperor, the central figure in the Middle Kingdom. For companies wanting to do business there, they need to be aware of this historical make-up of a country. You cannot unravel thousands of years of tradition in a decade.

The vectors of change – economics

The end of state dependency – the privatization of welfare

This vector will be relevant to gaining insights to the future of products and services where the customer's choice is heavily influenced by the need to provide independently for welfare. If you are in the business of health provision, insurance, pensions, savings, and other assurance related services then the implications for the likely privatization of welfare will be highly relevant to your future scenarios.

Highlights

- *Ageing population in developed world*
- *Efficiencies in health provision*
- *Extension in life expectancy*
- *Private insurance for high-risk groups*
- *Care for the elderly*
- *Savings*
- *The Gingrich phenomenon*

■ An ageing population

The developed world will continue to get older whilst the developing world will be younger than ever. More than half the world's population today is under 20 years of age and 90 percent of them live in the poorer developing world. This is 50 times the number of teenagers around in the baby boom years of the 1950s.

In the developed world, where in some countries the number of children per couple has fallen to below the 2.1 average needed to sustain a population, the number of people over 65 will grow steadily from around 14 percent to nearly 25 percent in some countries. Japan and Germany fare the worst in this area. Of every four people of working age one person will need to be supported. In fact the trend towards early retirement at 50 and the extension in life expectancy to 90 years makes the situation worse.

Ageing population is not only a developed country phenomenon. China, with its one child per couple policy, will have 22 percent of its population over the age of 60 by 2030, and Singapore, Thailand, Taiwan, and South Korea also face a similar situation.

The most immediate problem facing governments in the rich developed world will be the increasing demands for the provision of pensions, housing, health, and other services to the elderly. The current levels of service afforded to the elderly will almost certainly not be sustainable as more and more of them join their ranks. Many countries

The current levels of service afforded to the elderly will almost certainly not be sustainable.

in the developed world face a worrying problem of unfunded pensions liability, and there is no evidence that governments have made public the extent of the problem. Italy's future generations, for example, would need to pay five times more in taxation to maintain the existing level of benefit.

Of the US federal budget, 33 percent is currently for the benefit of the elderly. This is due to increase to 43 percent by the turn of the century. Organizations such as AARP (American Association for Retired Persons) lobby hard for new hospitals and upgraded facilities for the elderly. These are being given precedence over schools and education for the young, and younger citizens are begining to feel that their older politicians are selling their futures down the river. An organization called Lead or Leave, with some 20,000 members, wants the young to burn their social security cards in an effort to stress the extravagance of the older genera-

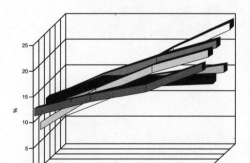

% over age 65
Source: OECD

Countries
☐ Japan ▨ US ■ Germany ■ UK ▨ Italy ▨ France

tions. This represents an enormous opportunity to the private sector as insurance companies are increasingly being relied upon to market and provide for the needs of the ageing population.

There is currently a trickle of products on the market aimed at the over-50 age group, and companies will face buying resistance, particularly in Europe, where the state has so far been able to support the aged. Over the next decade these attitudes will begin to change as populations in the developed world witness a gradual decline in the support from national institutions.

Lifetime taxation per person
Source: The Economist

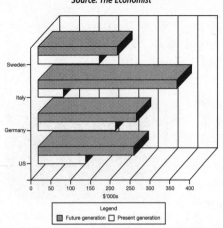

Legend
▨ Future generation □ Present generation

The services sector has so far been slow in targeting elderly people. We will gradually see a change in awareness of ageing customers' needs. Age Concern, a UK-based charity, recently launched a campaign aimed at retailers to heighten awareness of the difficulties the elderly face when in supermarkets. It asked executives to go shopping after putting on safety spectacles smeared with grease and tying weights to their arms and legs. This was an attempt to simulate partial blindness and arthritis, a condition faced by many old people. The trial showed how difficult it was for the elderly to reach the top of supermarket shelves and to read labels giving pricing information.

> The health system is one which will continue to attract attention and debate.

Forty-three percent of the US federal budget will be devoted to the elderly by the turn of the century.

■ Efficiencies in health provision

As the shrinking world promotes the comparison of company, country, and regional performance we will begin to examine and seek to emulate parts of the world which have more efficient forms of organization. The health system is one which will continue to attract attention and debate because for many countries it accounts for over 10 percent of GDP, the US and Switzerland being two of the highest spenders on health. In the US, which accounts for 40 percent of the world pharmaceutical market, this rate of expenditure is being questioned as about 20 percent of its population are not covered by mainstream health provision.

By and large, countries that provide for health through the private sector do not do so as efficiently as countries that provide cover through the state sector funded by taxation. Whether this is a function of state systems having economies of scale or the fact that private health providers have been less rigorous about challenging costs is not clear. It is likely, however, that privately funded health systems will put their expenditure much more under scrutiny in the future. Many have done so already. In the US, companies, via their managed care operations, are putting pressure on health providers to reduce costs with, for example, a move towards cheaper generic drug prescriptions wherever possible.

There have been calls in the House of Representatives to limit the power of the 9000-strong Federal Drug Administration (FDA), which, the pharmaceutical companies say, introduces unnecessary costs and delays into the granting of approvals for drugs and medical devices.

Health % of GDP

Source: OECD

■ Life expectancy

The advancement of medicine and improved living conditions have brought about an increase in life expectancy in countries around the world. In the developed world people live, on average, 25 years longer than they did at the turn of the century, and with recent breakthroughs in genetic engineering and the treatment of cancer we may be at the beginning of another stepwise increment in life expectancy. This may make the 100-year-old a common occurrence and add to the problem of ageing populations and the demands on care for the elderly.

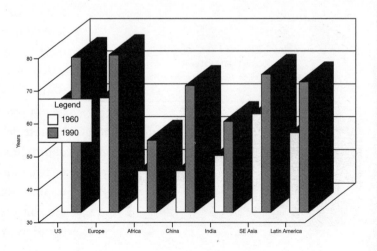

Life expectancy 1960–1990

As our life expectancy has continued to increase over the last 50 years, doctors are asking the question, "Is there an eventual age limit to our living?" Dr Michel Allard, a French researcher of the lives of centenarians, claims that we are already on the way to seeing the 150-year-old. The French average life expectancy has been going up consistently by three months every year and there are 30 times more centenarians now than there were 40 years ago. The search for anti-ageing products which deccelerate the complex ageing process is a multibillion research industry.

■ Private insurance for high-risk groups

With genetic research advancing the understanding of a person's disposition to certain diseases, it will be possible to predict an individual's life expectancy and vulnerability to disease. Cancer, heart conditions, and muscle-wasting diseases can be detected at birth.

There has been some concern expressed as to whether insurance companies may use DNA testing as a means of assessing premiums or indeed excluding certain groups from cover. Already companies charge additional premiums for families with a history of heart disease or other forms of ailment.

■ Care for the elderly

With an ageing society, the percentage of expenditure spent on care for the over-65s will increase. Much of this increase in expenditure will probably come from the private sector as most state systems are unlikely to meet the increase in resources required to fund the needs of the ageing population. Both France's and Germany's state health systems are already amongst the highest in the world, and with an approximate doubling of the elderly population over the next 20 years it is unlikely that companies or individuals are going to accept a substantial rise in taxation to fund these increases.

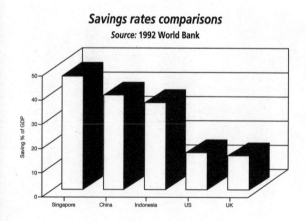

Savings rates comparisons
Source: 1992 World Bank

■ Savings

It is unclear whether saving to income ratios are more to do with cultural stereotypes or the need for security in later years. The Chinese, Singaporeans, and Indonesians are some of the highest savers, whilst the Anglo-Saxons are amongst the lowest. Some politicians argue that while people feel that the state will support them in times of hardship they are less likely to save for old age, sickness, or loss of income. As financial insecurity has risen in the West, savings rates are beginning to increase.

■ The Gingrich phenomenon

Newt Gingrich, the US Speaker of the House of Representatives, has introduced a new complex blend of libertarianism in the economic debate of how the US should be managed in the next century. His recommendations, which were the lynchpin of the Republican Contract for America manifesto, are based on two main considerations. Firstly, he argues that the US is decaying from crime, violence, teenage pregnancy, and inner-city poverty because people have moved away from traditional values. Secondly, he believes that the information age will change the way wealth is created in the future and that the US must adapt to the idea that knowledge and information are the mainstay of future success. In brief his recommendations are as follows:

- A fundamental change in the educational system, reinforcing older traditional values of the Western tradition, morality, and personal responsibility, and rejecting newer multicultural values. People should take control of their own education by introducing a free market into education via a voucher system to purchase training as required. Technology would be used to impart new educational needs with the established universities and colleges being drastically overhauled.
- Dismantling the current welfare system, introducing a flat income tax, cutting federal spending by a third, and permanently balancing the federal budget.
- Transferring federal functions to states and major cities.

Brainstorming the consequences

Politician: I have heard Andrew Marr of *The Independent* argue that we are moving to a situation where governments are facilitators more than doers. The private/public partnership is causing a revolution in education.

Sociologist: Also, more information is becoming public about schools' performances. The shrinking world has given rise to the benchmarking effect and we are beginning to measure our educational performance against a number of other countries. We compare low maths scores in the West with extraordinarily high scores in the East where they have far fewer teaching resources. Some Japanese educationalists are calling for a Western model in some areas to encourage creativity and innovation in the young.

Technologist: So we are seeing increasing amounts of information independently of how it is propagated because of the free market approach? This then enables people to make more choices, which can be confusing to the uninformed citizen who gets most of his or her views from some tabloid newspaper.

Sociologist: Yes, take for example people's views on job creation or Workfare, it is variable. Those who have built up an historical dependence on the state to provide employment rely heavily on such schemes. The growing band of self-employed hate the idea. Interestingly, Sweden has one of the toughest unemployment regimes, which is focussed very hard on getting people back to work. Unemployment is not an option. So the welfare system is for those who cannot work.

Economist: It is somewhat the same in Germany, where social and inter-generational obligations work. It is much clearer that parents and children have mutual responsibilities. It is duty and responsibility as well as claim and benefit.

Marketeer: On East/West values it is interesting to think that Japan is more like Germany in that they build infrastructure for the benefit of their citizens. They are empire builders: they invest today for the future, like Sweden. Whereas the Anglo-Saxon cultures borrow from tomorrow for today. There are different forces of play in these countries. In places like Sweden they pay high taxes and grumble but they understand why. This comes naturally – could it be transplanted? Probably not; we appear to be moving away from state responsibility to individual responsibility. Not many people outside Sweden want its system. Can you imagine any of the Asian countries feeling comfortable about a system of 70 percent taxation?

Economist: Maybe with health the emphasis should shift from cure to prevention. This has to be a key role for the state with an ageing population where the biggest proportion of expenditure occurs in the last few weeks of your life. Promoting healthy eating, taking regular exercise, tackling overweight, restrictions on smoking and drugs, and so on could significantly reduce the health bill later in life.

Author: Chile apparently has transformed its welfare system in a way that is favored by many. It appears to be a case study in managing change from state to private sector.

Economist: You know the word everyone has avoided is EUTHANASIA. Do the trends we are looking at point inexorably to saying that the entitlement to old age will have to be limited?

The vectors of change – economics

The transformation of work

The nature of work is an important consideration when developing scenarios for the providers of business services. A provider of information systems solutions will need to understand how employees might be dispersed geographically, while a bank serving small entrepreneurs might need to anticipate an expansion in one-person enterprises. These are some of the major influences discussed in this chapter.

Highlights

- *Manufacturing – drift to a low-wage world*
- *Jobs – the high ground*
- *The end of the "job"*
- *Youth unemployment*
- *Rise of economic diasporas*
- *The jobs backlash*

Popular themes

The end of the job? Manufacturing's drift to cheaper areas of labor – South-East Asia, Eastern Europe. The assault on white-collar jobs. The Virtual Corporation. Teleworking. The resilience of service industries. The rise in invisibles. Valuing intangible assets. The move to value-added. GATT and other mechanisms to protect jobs.

■ Manufacturing

Over the last 20 years the percentage of GDP arising from manufacturing and the volume of related employment has dwindled in the developed world in favor of services. Some countries like Germany and Japan remain more heavily committed to the manufacturing sector with 40 percent of GDP.

Britain, the US, and France have around 30 percent of their GDP in manufacturing and have moved substantially towards services.

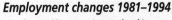

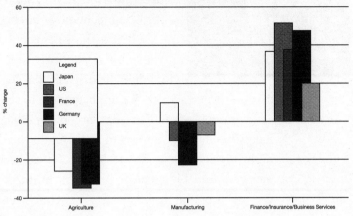

Jobs too have seen a drift away from the factory towards the services sector. Manufacturing jobs have been hardest hit because of automation and competition on labor costs from the developing world. Switzerland's factory labor costs at $28/hour and Germany's $25/hour seem unsustainable in comparison to China's estimated labor costs of between 50 cents and one dollar an hour.

In Basle, an executive from Ciba-Geigy's dye manufacturing unit based there explains the problem: "We are having to compete with dyes manufactured to the same quality and specification in South-East Asia at one-twentieth of the cost at which we can produce." Looking around at the workers in the Basle plant, who clearly reflect a relatively relaxed and affluent lifestyle compared to their peers in Shanghai or Seoul, one wonders how much longer their jobs are sustainable given the existing disparity.

> **Germany and Japan are going to be vulnerable to competition from cheaper manufacturing labor markets.**

Mercedes announced a 1995 agreement with the PRC to manufacture a compact car in China and later in 1996 signed a similar agreement in Brazil. By beating off a number of their US rivals, Mercedes will be tapping into a booming Asian and South American market for a small quality car. Good news for Mercedes shareholders but little comfort for Mercedes car workers back home in Germany.

Hamish McRae in his book *The world in 2020* argues that both Germany and Japan are going to be vulnerable to competition from cheaper manufacturing labor markets in the developing world. Those countries more reliant on services will be able to weather the competition of cheaper labor cost because most services do not cross national or geographic boundaries easily. You have to care for the sick and elderly at or near where they live. You have to serve fast food near where the consumer wants it. Industrial countries have difficulty in preserving an advantage because technical innovation passes

> **With information-related services we are beginning to see significant cross-border labor competition.**

quickly from one country to another. PC clones are produced in most Asian countries today. Japanese car manufacturing technology has been emulated in the UK.

Whereas this rule would apply in certain service sectors where physical distribution or local tastes and preferences confine the delivery to a country's boundaries, with information-related services we are beginning to see significant cross-border labor competition. An Indian software programmer at Tata's software unit in Bangalore may be charged to a client at around $10 an hour compared with his or her equivalent in Palo Alto at $80 an hour. What's more, the programmer will probably be more proficient in the currently demanding C++ and C+++ programing languages. General Electric, American Express, and a host of other multinationals have been using Indian software factories in preference to service providers in their home markets.

> **"1985–93 only 6 percent of people changed sector. Real shifts were to more skilled jobs in sector"**
>
> *Manpower OECD countries*

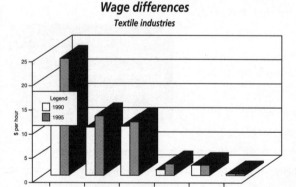

Wage differences
Textile industries

Cheap networking and communications should make it possible to move most information-oriented services to anywhere in the world where labor costs are competitive and where language and cultural preferences are not a barrier. Baxter's, the healthcare company, has moved its back office administration and accounting activities across the border to Mexico to take advantage of cheap labor and an ample supply of educated, English-speaking workers.

> **If the developed world is to protect jobs then it will do so with "value added" activities.**

■ Jobs, the high ground

If the developed world is to protect jobs then it will do so with "value added" activities in areas where a country or a company is seen to have extraordinary competencies. Michael Porter in his work on the Competitive Advantage of Nations argued that countries were at their best when they concentrated on what they did best. Thus the Taiwanese and Japanese have developed competencies in electronics which the French or Germans, say, would be ill-advised to compete with. Germans on the other hand have a reputation for designing and building reliable machines while the United States has taken the high ground in communications.

Top FX financial centers
Source: Bank for International Settlements

London, New York, and Tokyo are the world's three top financial centers, despite sky-high accommodation and white-collar labor costs. Yet despite these barriers the world's major financial institutions congregate in these cities because proximity to others in the financial community still counts for something. It adds value. These cities will remain competitive as long as they add value as a financial market.

A 1995 survey put London as the leading trading center in the global foreign exchange market. Over 80 percent of the business conducted was by international institutions, and both dollar and yen transactions dominated over sterling business. Companies chose London because they believed that the market there was liquid, orderly, and international.

True World Cities like London compete for global business. They may become the competitive advantage of nations.

Hollywood will continue to be the film capital of the world as long as US culture and its associated images portrayed by the producers remain attractive to the millions of people around the world. The manufacturing cost of a compact disc is less than 5 percent of the cost at the point of sale. We can press discs anywhere in the world, but the creative content on the disc, its marketing and promotion, and the image projected by the artist are not areas which are subject to labor competition.

Brands too, play an important part in protecting jobs, provided companies continue to invest in building up their brands. Pat Mann, a director of international brand management at JWT, says, "Companies have been living off the legacy of their brands without putting anything back."

"Companies have been living off the legacy of their brands without putting anything back."

Loss-making Adidas, the German sports company, chose ex-Saatchi marketeer Robert Louis-Drefus to get it back on the rails. One of his first actions was to move manufacturing out to Asia in order to cut manufacturing costs and allow the company to concentrate on building the brand and introduce new technology into their sports shoes.

The growth of Singapore and Hong Kong has been largely due to their status as trading posts.

Whatever a country produces, be they services or goods, the only way most countries can support its citizens to a reasonable standard of living is by being able to earn income from exports. The growth of services, or invisibles as they are sometimes referred to, has been steadily growing. Countries like Britain have been earning more and more each year from invisibles instead of from manufactured goods. And the growth of Singapore and Hong Kong has been largely due to their status as trading posts.

The jobs therefore that we would deviate towards in the next 20 years would be those in the higher value-added service industries as traditional labor-intensive manufacturing gets pushed out to lower-wage economies or automated. Some of these service industries have been around for a while, some may not have yet been created. Marketing, distribution, media and communications, healthcare, and leisure are the established areas where the developed world will continue to grow new jobs. The emerging professions such as financial advisers, management consultancy, and broking of commodities, stocks, and currencies will be areas which will enjoy substantial export potential.

■ The end of the job

Employment as we know it today is about 150 years old and is the product of the industrialization of work. There are, however, a number of factors affecting jobs as we know them. Probably three out of four jobs today could be automated or reengineered. Organizations have only begun to scratch the surface of making productivity improvements using technology. White-collar jobs would take the most significant cuts in the next decade. Japan, although the most efficient in its factory processes, is way behind its competitor countries in making white-collar productivity improvements.

> *Probably three out of four jobs today could be automated or reengineered.*

Automation has traditionally sought to automate the scarcest resource. The use of intelligent systems, and the development of neural networks and Cyc, a type of knowledge-based computing, could eventually reduce the need for some of the more expensive professions. Thus tax advisers, general practitioners, legal counsel, and other similar interpretative professions could be affected by advanced expert systems. Already the accounting profession is having to redesign the entire business of auditing to pass on to clients the advantages of automated transaction systems.

> *As industries continue to consolidate we should see further job reductions in the pharmaceutical, car manufacturing, food, and airline industries.*

Company mergers and de-mergers are displacing jobs. When Sweden's Pharmacia and the US Upjohn merged they announced that 4,000 jobs would be axed. Glaxo/Wellcome announced the loss of 9,000 jobs from their merger, and Chase Manhattan and Chemical Bank said that their merger would shed 12,000 jobs. AT&T announced that it will be cutting 40,000 jobs following it spinning off its computer business. Since their original spin off from AT&T, the Baby Bells have shed 150,000 jobs. As industries continue to consolidate we should see further job reductions in the pharmaceutical, car manufacturing, food, and airline industries.

> *Future work patterns will be a "portfolio" of different contracts or relationships with companies.*

There is a school of thought, led most notably by Charles Handy, which suggests that future work patterns will be a "portfolio" of different contracts or relationships with companies. There is evidence that this trend has already begun, particularly with large corporations that have terminated full-time contracts of employment with their older managers and issued them with renewable consultancy contracts.

A portfolio pattern of working emerges after someone has spent the early part of their working life with a company, gaining essential work experience and finding out what they do particularly well. Portfolio working may not be confined only to knowledge workers but also to skill-based and manually intensive jobs where this arrangement has been operating for hundreds of years. Many of us don't need full-time window-cleaners or builders or graphic designers, but we need their services on a reliable periodic basis. In rural communities people often take on a number of different skills to spread their job net wider. Someone may, for example, repair cars in the busy summer and drive trucks in the winter.

The spate of downsizing initiatives by corporations has displaced numbers of well-qualified economists who have found themselves having to work as consultants, freelance analysts, or entrepreneurial publishers. Companies are finding it more cost-effective to buy specialist independent analytical services when they need them. A consensus forecast, available by subscription, for a particular market may cost $500–$1,000, but probably a year's work for an economist on, say, $100,000 per annum. With those economics the company finds it more effective to buy rather than hire. The challenge for the freelancer, speculatively compiling a forecast, is whether he or she will be successful in selling enough forecasts to pay for the time. As with most people moving from full-time employment with a single employer, life as a self-employed professional is more insecure, and after a long career of having been assured a monthly pay cheque, the transition to a variable income can be difficult.

> *Portfolio working will require people to develop a new mind-set of multi-tasking and building relationships with more than one employer.*

> *The job-for-life promises made by the likes of IBM in the 1980s are unlikely to return.*

Portfolio working will require people to develop a new mind-set of multi-tasking and building relationships with more than one employer. This is the service culture at its most sophisticated. The growing number of people who work in consulting roles these days will be best equipped to handle these working arrangements.

Although portfolio working will increase, these forms of working relationship are unlikely to be the norm for the majority of employment arrangements as most organizations will need full-time employees for some time to come. Several company roles, from the receptionist to the president, will remain full-time roles, and these positions will increasingly become more valued than part-time or temporary arrangements. The job-for-life promises made by the likes of IBM in the 1980s are unlikely to return and we may get more companies entering into renewable contractual relationships for senior executives and more junior operatives.

The continuing globalization of companies will call for employees who are not only prepared to spend most of their careers away from the home office but also have an international outlook in their attitudes and educational training. Companies which operate in global markets will increasingly introduce a greater cultural mix of senior executives to their senior management ranks to reflect the markets in which they operate.

The arrival of the leisure society postulated 20 years ago is unlikely to materialize. Jeff Mulgan of Demos, a UK think tank, says, "People love to work; the need to work is a natural part of our lives. The time-rich are usually money-poor and can't afford leisure. Those that can afford leisure get less time every year to enjoy it." The Henley Centre estimates that the average time for leisure has actually fallen from 23 hours per week in 1970 to 17.5 hrs in 1990.

> *"People love to work; the need to work is a natural part of our lives.*

The anxiety amongst people about employment has continued to rise, with most people feeling uncertain about their job. This will continue until people get used to more temporary employer–employee relationships over the next decade. It is unlikely that legislation in European states will be strengthened to protect jobs as companies will react by relocating activities in countries where they have more flexibility of employment. Unemployment in the EU has reached as high as 23 percent in Spain with most countries recording levels well above 10 percent. A fifth of the under-25-year-olds are unemployed.

> *It is unlikely that legislation in European states will be strengthened to protect jobs as companies will react by relocating activities in countries where they have more flexibility of employment.*

■ Youth unemployment

Unemployment of the young in the developed world is perhaps the greatest cause for concern over the next 20 years. Within a generation the school leaver or college graduate has had his or her expectations changed from enjoying a greater than 90 percent certainty of employment to a less than 50 percent chance in some countries. In France, where hourly rates for the 18-year-old are the highest in the world, unemployment too is one of the highest in the developed world. Even in Japan, which has enjoyed full employment until recently, youth employment is believed to be as high as 20

> **It will become necessary to attract the over-50s into organizations.**

percent. In order to avoid expensive redundancy costs and keep within the tough legislation protecting existing workers, new recruitment has been cut back, further adding to the problem.

Corporations will also become aware that the resource pool of young people to employ will diminish and it will become necessary to attract the over-50s into organizations. It will give this age group increased earnings potential compared to their younger counterparts.

■ The rise of economic diasporas

People in countries with exploding populations will attempt to migrate to neighboring countries to seek work and economic prosperity. Countries particularly under pressure from this migration will be South Africa, the Mediterranean countries which border North Africa, and the United States experiencing flows of people from Mexico and further south from Latin America.

> **Countries will become increasingly vigilant in policing their borders.**

Receiving countries will become increasingly vigilant in policing their borders in order to protect the standards of living for their own citizens. For countries such as South Africa with its land-based borders this will present a problem. The countries in the European Union will not feel comfortable with borderless controls and they will continue to accuse each other of lax procedures. The pressure on national identity cards throughout the EU will increase despite opposition from civil liberty groups.

In response to pressure from nationalist groups, in 1995, France stepped up its repatriation of illegal immigrants, many of them North Africans, to a target of 24,000 per annum. Chartered aircraft are used to carry out this large-scale exercise which has increased deportations by more than three times previous levels. Pat Buchanan, a Republican US presidential hopeful, called for the "fencing off" of Mexico in an effort to halt immigration.

Some countries such as the United States will exploit cheap migrant labor to support its labor intensive services sector where the current average wage is under $3/hour, well below the minimum wage in the most of Europe. Koreans in California keep open convenience stores 24 hours a day, and Russians and Asians do the unenviable job of driving New York taxis around the congested city. In Britain, immigrants from the Caribbean, and more recently the Philippines, have provided a cheap source of labor in areas such as the health service and care for the elderly, whilst Asians and Turks have regenerated the rag trade in the sweatshops of London and the Midlands.

Countries will also selectively wish to attract migrants for both economic and skill reasons. These migrations, now being labeled economic diasporas, will be enticed by the enhanced earning capacity in the developed world and the ability to reverse some of this income back into their own countries. We see Australia positively encouraging migrants from Asia in an attempt to attract some of the estimated one million Chinese dollar millionaires in the region. The one million Indians working in the US are estimated to have an average earnings level of $85,000 per annum, one of the highest of any ethnic grouping, and the ten million migrant Indians worldwide are collectively worth $350 billion according to *Business Week*. The government of India offers preferred investment conditions to these migrants in an effort to attract some of this capital.

> **Countries will also selectively wish to attract migrants for both economic and skill reasons.**

■ The jobs backlash

The strike in the autumn of 1995 at Boeing in Seattle illustrates the opposition of workers in the West to the export of jobs to the developing world. Workers who are asked to train their Asian counterparts so that they can establish similar practices back at home are resenting and sometimes refusing to do so. Robert Reich, US secretary of state for labor, is behind a plan to make it more difficult for companies like Boeing to bring into the country cheaper skilled labor for training. Similar antagonism is growing in computer programing where India and the Philippines provide a rich source of cheap programers and in cinematography where Europeans can be hired for less than half the rate of American professionals.

> **For at least the past decade we have had the idea before us that masses of people will be working from home.**

Teleworking

For at least the past decade we have had the idea before us that masses of people will be working from home and creating

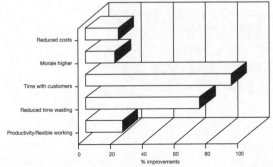

Improvements from teleworking
Source: Horack Adler Case Study

Reduced costs
Morale higher
Time with customers
Reduced time wasting
Productivity/flexible working

0   20   40   60   80   100
% improvements

a new teleworking culture. It has not happened, for some of the following reasons. Employers have been generally ambivalent about the idea. A trial, say, with a select few who have expressed the desire to work from home because of family commitments has to be terminated because other employees resent the special treatment.

Although most teleworking trials report an increase in productivity, most managers find it hard to assess the work output of employees if they are not actually on the premises. As the saying goes, "Success is 80 percent about turning up." Being there seems to be important to employers.

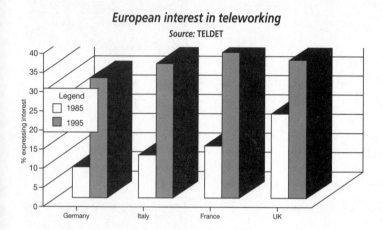

European interest in teleworking
Source: TELDET

Man is a social animal. In the workplace, the chance conversation by the coffee machine, the accidental interchange in the corridor, or the conviviality of the evening drink in a nearby bar can all contribute to networking and understanding work colleagues in a way that electronic communications fail to do.

But there are other forces which may make teleworking a more universal form of work. Overhead costs in most organizations are being challenged and unit heads are being asked to examine all means of reducing cost. With office costs in most major cities of the world at around $100 a square foot fully loaded, the cost of accommodating an employee is $10,000 per annum. With a hundred employees on the premises the organization could be spending a million avoidable dollars.

> **The office in its present form is probably the worst utilized asset in the company.**

Various studies have indicated that many employees spend less than 9 percent of the total time in the office (based on the assumption that the facility is available 100 percent of the time). The office in its present form is probably the worst utilized asset in the company. Digital telecommunications are making it more possible for employees to pass documents, mail, and conduct video conferencing from remote locations as if they were in the office next door. With the increasing internationalization of businesses, more communication is conducted out of the office and across time zones. Being in the office from 9 to 5 becomes less relevant.

With a move to portfolio working, described under the section on work, an employer does not always expect attendance at the workplace. In fact there probably wouldn't be a place for you in the office if you did turn up.

If more and more people turn to teleworking then they will require special work spaces built into their homes. Many make do with inappropriate work space – the converted garden shed or the closet under the stairs. Alternatively, communities may organize communal business centers where people can work from and share the costs of secretarial cover and other infrastructure-related expenditure. Some telecommunication companies have begun to offer "hot cottage" communication facilities in rural locations. Equally banks may offer their increasingly redundant local branches as neighbourhood teleworking centers as an extension of their services to small businesses and portfolio workers.

Whereas the car today is included as a fringe benefit, for many employees we may see the introduction of the teleworking package as a future fringe benefit to encourage employees to work away from the office. More senior personnel would have a "deluxe" package which would include a contribution towards business center expenses, while others may be offered a basic PC with connections.

With more people working from home, expect to see a rise in "communitarianism," as people spend more time in their neighborhood communities. People's need for status and recognition will come from within the community rather than their place of work. Without the split between work and the home, individuals will place more importance on issues of the environment and business ethics says Andy Law, Chairman of St Lukes in London.

The realization that office space is an inefficient use of assets will accelerate the trend towards telecommuting. Photo: BT

The office – a wasted asset
Source: Birchall/Adams

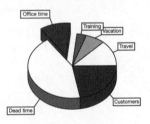

> **Banks may offer their increasingly redundant local branches as neighbourhood teleworking centres.**

> **We may see the introduction of the teleworking package as a future fringe benefit.**

The take-up of teleworking as a way of life may be more successful in individualistic cultures such as the US and Northern Europe. In more collectivist cultures the social needs met in the workplace may result in a slower take-up of people working from home.

> The new world of work:
>
> There are those who are working
> There are those who are looking for work
> There are those who have given up
> There are those who have never had the opportunity to work
>
> *David Arkless – VP Manpower*

For individuals working on their own the need for marketing their skills to assure continued employment will become increasingly important. As one trainer in IT skills pointed out, "We spend all our time working and as a consequence have very little time for marketing ourselves. At the end of a contract we have a gap of several weeks when we have to get out and find work."

Outsourcing and the virtual organization

Manpower, the organization which provides resources to companies on a temporary basis, is today the world's biggest employer, placing two million people a year in jobs. Its growth and success is partly borne out of the need for individuals to have someone else do their marketing and partly by the growth in outsourcing and the "virtual" organization.

Consultants have postulated a future where the world will be populated by "virtual" companies which subcontract all their activities, bar the central corporate governance functions.

Outsourcing is the term used to define a company that contracts out some of its non-core activities to other organizations who through economies of scale and increased specialization can perform those activities more efficiently. Thus a company like EDS runs GM's computer systems and Price Waterhouse manages some of British Petroleum's accounting systems. Some governments such as that in the UK have contracted out a range of services from garbage collection to prison operations to security firms. Some management consultants have postulated a future where the world will be populated by "virtual" companies which subcontract all their activities, bar the central corporate governance functions.

Manpower's operations now cover a wide spectrum of activities. When Philips wanted 100 PhDs for three months, Manpower sourced 90 percent of those required from advertising on the Internet. Hewlett Packard wanted to rotate its researchers out of the company to get fresh brains and ideas. Manpower took on the job by employing R&D personnel who swapped places with peers at institutions like Stanford for a period of time before being recycled back into *HP*'s research labs. Manpower also employs the entire 2,000 workforce at a US *HP* manufacturing facility, runs IBM's maintenance, installation, and customer service operation in the UK, and runs the 500 sales-force for Dainippon's printing operations.

Microsoft divulged that MCI, the telecommunications company, had been asked to run the entire customer service operation of its new online service, a deal valued at around $20 million a year.

Brainstorming the consequences

Is this the knowledge era?

Strategist: You need to distinguish between services and knowledge-based buinesses. Service is a business that requires the customer to create the product. That does not apply necessarily to knowledge, which is something that can't be stored on a shelf.

There is a better way of looking at it: low-value-added vs high-value-added work. Or physical manufacture vs knowledge work. Can you separate these and still maintain the knowledge aspect? Can we allow cars to be made completely out of Europe? Could we have software designed here but constructed in the Philippines?

Economist: Is this not already happening? And anyway, is not the Third World already capturing some of the knowledge high ground?

Politician: Look at the UK car industry. Most Formula One cars are made and designed in the UK, while the mass industry has disappeared – except where foreigners come and make it work. So on the one hand there is the ability to do some very sophisticated engineering work, but on the other we are hopeless at managing local people in a manufacturing process. It is all the same job after all.

Sociologist: Is the answer for countries/regions to become specialist knowledge centers like Silicon Valley? Does it make a difference where the profits go? For example, the center of TV-making expertise is in Japan, but France has nonetheless kept a grip on TV expertise by manufacturing, albeit not as profitably as Japan.

Author: What about the problem of the ageing population? What effect will this have on work?

Politician: There is a scarcity of talented people and we cannot afford early retirement of skilled people. We have to use those skills in perhaps different roles. Also, people are retiring earlier and will need to earn an income.

Actor: Why not get your degree when you are older and start work when you are 18?

Economist: Yeh, we could even encourage multi-skilling: have skills, will travel.

Politician: For the first time we have 20–30 years of post-working life. What do you do with these millions? What products do they want and need?

Author: I wonder if we should brainstorm two opposing themes. How about one where we *decouple* the process of manufacture from the design or knowledge creation, and the other a world where we keep the entire process *integrated* and tightly coupled.

Decoupling manufacturing from design and knowledge creation

Strategist: We are assuming here that we are no longer required to be in control of the process steps-sourcing, etc. We focus on core competencies and know our business/customers and educate our suppliers and manufacturers. We also have the greatest flexibility in growing or contracting the business depending on demand.

Technologist: There are a number of organizational methods to employ, some enabled by information technology, such as franchising, electronic distribution channels, and the encouragement of entrepreneurs.

Economist: Decoupling demands capital flexibility – companies can take advantage of capital markets around the world. Also decentralization can create new sources of capital via devices such as franchising.

Strategist: Decoupling gives access to a portfolio of suppliers and outlets. You can create a core of people working closely and identifying with you – a portfolio of suppliers/outlets. But you need to exercise an element of control or structure in place, like McDonald's does with its tightly defined retailing systems.

Marketeer: It helps to bring about best practices more quickly because you are dealing with a wider domain of companies who may also be trading with other companies. Your packaging supplier may be dealing, with P&G or Phillip Morris, say, who tend to continue to push their suppliers to provide higher and higher standards of performance.

Sociologist: It creates skills centers. You can hire people at locations where there is an abundance of good-quality skills, and that means a finer definition of skills. In Moscow recently there was a mass availability of ex-rocket scientists at very affordable rates: an excellent opportunity for someone to set up a technical R&D capability in, say, avionics. We may see more of this in the future. Although companies would have to be flexible about locating parts of their key operations where these high-caliber-knowledge workers want to live. If Palo Alto is where your top software designers want to live then you'd best be thinking about basing your software design skills center there.

Economist: Taxation will be also be a key driver for locating one's operations, both from the point of view of personal and corporate taxation. Ireland's favorable tax regime for overseas companies and for certain categories of professional have acted like a magnet for many US and Japanese companies.

Strategist: You can begin to see a move from what is currently a broadly based service sector to a service and high knowledge sector.

Author: We can see here the creation of large virtual companies. But the satellites would need access to certain expertise at the core. My distributor in a maturing market would need assistance from the center to understand where the company has previously experienced a similar maturation and what the appropriate response might be.

Politician: Lots of jobs presumably for corporate lawyers to establish control processes by creating a legal framework, using fixed-term contracts.

Journalist: You can imagine a growth in extensive networks of smaller offices and temporary/interim business centers in hotels and similar establishments.

Sociologist: This will undoubtedly mean an increase in high-quality career counselling. If you are caught in a skills trap, i.e. your skills quickly become commoditized or redundant, you'll have one hell of a job finding work. We should also expect a higher-stressed life and therefore may need more emotional stability to cope. A regular visit to the shrink may become essential.

Marketeer: This could require some creative thinking on behalf of personal finance providers and those supplying risk insurance. With more uncertainty about regarding one's future employment prospects, presumably flexible schemes would need to operate, i.e. higher premiums for people while in work and lower premiums while not in work.

Actor: Yes, just like us actors have had to make do for as long as I can remember – the "resting" actor, and all that.

Sociologist: This will also mean greater multiculturalism in the working groups and the communities we live in. Like the Japanese communities that live in clusters around London or New York. Global managers may only spend a fraction of their time living and working in the city where they were born and bred.

Author: This also means that global transport and communications increase substantially as people spend a considerable amount of time keeping in touch with the various disparate parts of the organization

Opposing theme:
Integrated knowledge and manufacturing kept tightly coupled

(from the point of view of a US CEO)

Author: In this theme, companies keep control of knowledge generation and the production process in a tightly coupled organizational structure. The assumption is that if you aren't a closely integrated company then you lose control to your competitors. An oil company, for example, would feel the need to closely manage all its activities from wellhead to customer, a computer manufacturer would keep close control of technical development, manufacturing, and distribution.

Marketeer: As a US CEO you have a concern that wage costs may have gone through the roof at home. Although the quality of subcontractors in, say, Central Europe is fine, they also work for competitors. One answer is to set up a subsidiary and pay over the odds, or fragment roles to maintain control (also, tie in with things like bonuses and share option, and loyalty contracts).

Economist: The company would almost certainly keep R&D and marketing at the center with skills and competencies at the home office. Jobs at the center would be career jobs, probably for near life durations, and with minimal input from other centers of excellence in subsidiaries or other countries. Jobs outside the center would be deskilled in order to keep control. Thus for a software company the key competence of design and maintenance of the source code would be done at the center. Distribution of the software and sales support, a relatively lower-skilled set of activities, may be handled by subsidiaries, run and managed by locals.

Marketeer: The high balance of power at the core might create instability? You might have to work harder to keep control of subsidiaries. If these subs were in economies which were booming themselves then they might regard themselves as second grade.

Politician: The company would almost certainly use retainers and have non-compete clauses for non-subsidiaries.

Marketeer: The role of the country manager becomes almost honorific, becoming more involved in implementing HQ dictats, dealing with the country government and local customer complaints. Country people are "consulted" but never involved. It becomes more of a two-tier system.

Sociologist: Long-term education is important even outside the core, but it is more about skills training. Skills to learn quickly and structure thought processes. Concept creation is done at center. This becomes a problem with people being overly qualified outside the core, which is seen as a threat.

Author: Regional centres, run by expats, control groups of subsidiaries in adjoining countries. Regional center in, say, Paris controls Europe, Singapore controls South-East Asia.

Marketeer: The integrated company attempts to create single global brands to impose a world view based on central ideology and to get economies of scale. Also, other suppliers get bigger as HQ wants to deal with more centralized companies who share culture. Thus we see a single ad agency handling a global account with some sacrifice of quality and creativity.

Author: A big downside of this theme is that innovation is reduced – big centralized companies (and they will get bigger) have the resources but less incentive to innovate. There would be a less satisfying role for entrepreneurs, who need closer operating specifications and procedures.

Economist: However, they find it easier to manage things like company pensions and health insurance with employees in more long-term contracts of employment.

The vectors of change – economics

The haves and have-nots

Social trends are of interest to all consumer product companies, retailers and service organizations dealing with the end-consumer. The more that society separates itself into the haves and have-nots, the greater the delineation of consumer values. Price is sacrificed at the expense of quality for the majority, brands become status symbols for those that "have" and market segmentation is often along tribal lines. Here we look at how this vector of change has begun to manifest itself in the world today.

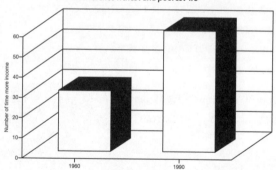

World population income changes
Difference richest and poorest 1/5

Highlights

- *The two-tier society*
- *The demographic time bomb*
- *Third World debt*
- *Growth*
- *The gap widens*
- *Tribalism – ethnoscapes*

■ The two-tier society

Over the last 20 years in most of the developed world the gap between the rich and poor has widened and nowhere else is this more pronounced than in the United States, where in cities like Los Angeles the gated estates of the rich are located within spitting distance of crime-ridden slums. Approximately 22 million US citizens live on private estates and five million live in security protected colonies. In the last 30 years the difference between the top one-fifth of the world's population and the poorest one-fifth has increased from 30 times to 60 times. Europe too has not escaped the widening gap, where over the last ten years the Henley Centre reports that the top 10 percent of UK earners have increased their income by 68 percent whilst the bottom 10 percent have actually lost earning capacity by 17 percent.

The British economist Robin Marris has segmented society into the "all rights," those with education and comfortable incomes, and the "low-eds," the under-educated underclass who live on income supplement or are unemployed. He maintains that without growth in the developed world, the underclass will continue to be subsidized by the privileged people who have jobs. Globalization will merely exacerbate the problem by exporting "low-ed" jobs to low-wage countries.

> *Without growth in the developed world, the underclass will continue to be subsidized by the privileged people.*

A couple of British academics, Prof. Tim Lang and Yannis Gabriel, in their book *The Unmanageable Consumer* highlight the inequalities of consumers. "While some consumers may spend inordinate amounts of time deliberating whether to invest in a new swimming pool, a new yacht, or a second home, others have to choose between feeding their children and buying them new shoes."

% income change 1980–1990
Source: Henley Centre

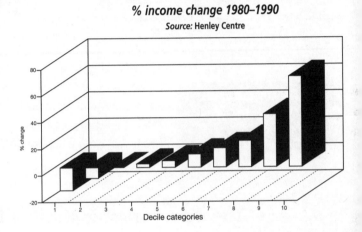

The European Union also appears to be heading towards a two-tier federation with an increasing separation between richer and poorer nations. Germany, France, and the Benelux countries frequently appear in the upper tier, while Britain, Ireland, and Spain occupy the lower tier. On a more global scale the poorer countries of Central Africa

> *Some need to choose between feeding their children and buying them new shoes.*

have GNPs less than the net profits made by corporations. A 1994 newspaper headline ran "What do Goldman Sachs and Zambia have in common?" The answer was that the 1993/94 $2.6bn earnings for the 160 partners of Goldman Sachs equaled the GNP of Zambia in the same year.

> *$2.6bn earnings for the 160 partners of Goldman Sachs equalled the GNP of Zambia.*

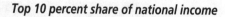

Top 10 percent share of national income
Source: World Bank

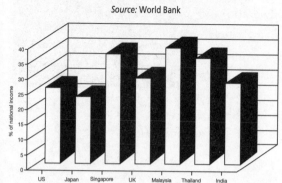

Relative income per head

Source: 1992 World Bank

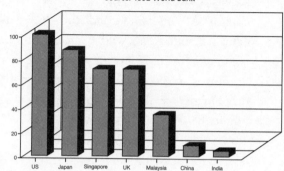

The emerging countries of South-East Asia, although now amongst the wealthiest in the world, have to cope with greater inequalities in their societies than in the developed world. Malaysia's inequality is almost double that of Japan's. Thailand and Singapore also have a high concentration of earners in the top 10 percent.

> **Malaysia's inequality is almost double that of Japan's.**

■ The demographic time bomb

Whichever way you look at the world over the next 20 years, population growth continues relentlessly. The current world population of just under six billion will be eight billion by the year 2020. Ninety percent of this growth will be in Asia, Latin America, and Africa. Africa will be the highest growth area, almost doubling its existing 750 million. Europe is virtually static at 0.5 billion, with the United States experiencing marginal growth of less than 1 percent per annum. Japan, like Europe, does not experience any net increase.

> **Africa will be the highest growth area, almost doubling its existing 750 million population.**

World population
Source: World Bank Population Survey

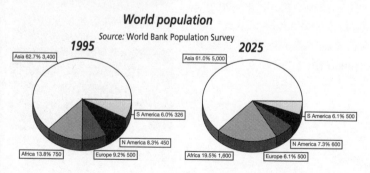

These figures represent significant drivers for change in the world. The developing world's increasing population pressures create more people in the developing world who come of working age and are available for work in the increasingly mobile labor markets of the world. In some parts of the world where population increases are unsustainable, tribal conflict, war, and genocide will stifle economic development and keep away corporations. The region of greatest vulnerability is Africa where neither natural resources, health provision, nor clean water can support a doubling in the existing population numbers.

> *Where population increases are unsustainable, tribal conflict, war, and genocide will stifle economic development.*

Third World debt

The World Bank is one of the major lenders to the Third World. The US Congress, which approves the country's major contributions to the bank, has threatened to scale back its future share.

There have been allegations that the bank's 11,000 employees have done little to help the Third World. This criticism comes also from ecology groups, who argue that many of the bank's policies in the 1970s and 1980s did more harm than good to poor countries. The bank has argued strongly in favour of its role and the importance of helping the developing world's growth. China, for example, is the bank's largest borrower. Many of its citizens earn less than a dollar a day and are at less than half the $600 per annum threshold set by the bank to qualify for lending.

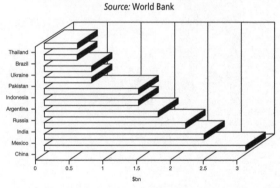

Ten largest borrowers – BRD/IDA lending

Source: World Bank

Countries such as Madagascar, Zaïre, Cameroon, Sudan, Somalia, and Angola have already got to a point where any serious economic analysis of their debt position would be impossible. The world's banking institutions will need to produce innovative mechanisms to save these countries from complete bankrupcy.

> *China, for example, is the bank's largest borrower. Many of its citizens earn less than a dollar a day.*

The World Bank has proposed a plan to relieve the $160 billion debt burden of the 40 poorest nations with the help of a $11 billion trust fund. The bank has some $17 billion in reserves, $1 billion in annual income, and a surplus account of around $850 million. Although the plan has a number of opponents in the world banking community, the new President of the World Bank, Mr James Wolfenson, has spoken of the need to come up with new solutions to solving the debt burden of the poorest countries, many of whom are in Africa. The need to maintain the liquidity of debtor nations will compete in future with funds required to provide aid to those same countries.

■ Growth

Growth is the strongest determinant of the success or failure of a country. If the growth hierarchy shown below is replicated over the next 25 years then the disposition of the world's largest economies looks very different from the way we know it today.

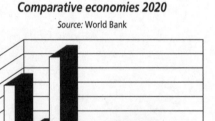

Comparative economies 2020
Source: World Bank

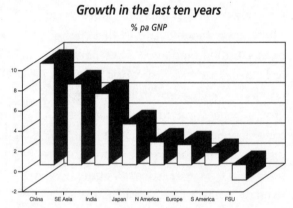

Growth in the last ten years
% pa GNP

If only by virtue of its sheer size, China becomes the world's largest economy, putting the United States into second place. Provided India changes its policies towards foreign investment, reduces red tape, and creates a more decentralized form of goverment, it could become the world's fourth-largest economy after Japan. Western suppliers have been clamoring at the doors of Chinese officials to get a share of the lucrative orders for goods and services which will be fuelled by this growth. Boeing and Airbus have been beneficiaries with billions in orders, and with promises by officials that China will be needing at least another 800 aircraft over the next 15 years. China's demand for air travel will grow at 10 percent per annum, twice the average growth rate.

> **China becomes the world's largest economy.**

Recently China's growth has slowed slightly, causing analysts to re-examine their projections about the world's most populous country, where 900 million of its 1.2 billion people live in relative poverty. China has unleashed a tremendous force for increasing the economic prosperity of its people. At risk is the political stability of the country. There is also a growing concern that the country will be unable to control inflation and that Western companies which have invested most heavily in the country may be at greatest risk. But China has not been the only country in the region to experience great growth.

At the end of 1995 the US announced its intention to end the General System of Privileges (GSP) to Malaysia. The GSP grants duty-privileges to developing countries whose economies the US wishes to encourage. The US now considers this country not only to be self-supporting but also a potential competitor for US products. Malaysia's own Proton cars and its production capability in electronic components for Motorola,

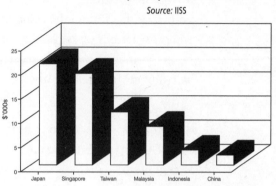

Relative per capita Asian income

Source: IISS

Intel, Texas Instruments, and other major producers has brought its per capita income close to the $8,000 threshold which the US uses as a barometer of eligibility for the GSP. In the words of a US trade representative, Malaysia had achieved an "extraordinary success."

Malaysia had achieved an "extraordinary success".

There are currently over 150 million credit card holders in Asia, accounting for $200 billion of consumer expenditure, twice that of three years ago. With some 800 million children under the age of 16, the credit card industry is expecting an even bigger boom as younger, more affluent consumers are more likely to embrace the "plastic" culture. Of the 50 million Indians who could potentially qualify for a

Reversal of fortunes

Developed nations' smaller output share

Legend
☐ Developing countries
▨ NICs
■ Industrialized countries

1984

1994

2004

credit card, only two million carry one. This represents a tremendous marketing opportunity for both local and international issuers.

GE Capital has been introducing the hire purchase mentality to Asia by helping consumers finance consumer durables such as washing machines, refrigerators, and other domestic appliances. The development of a database of credit worthy customers will no doubt give it an advantage in assessing future holders of its credit cards. And Asians are getting smart card technology ahead of US consumers as companies are test marketing the technology with groups of customers. Asia, with its large populations and an emerging middle class roughly equivalent to the size of Western Europe, will be an area of potentially high growth, provided the continent enjoys a reasonable degree of political stability.

The following key indicators provide clues as to the future of the region:

- China's attitude to Hong Kong post the 1997 takeover. If the colony is left to develop itself economically and continue to be the powerhouse of the region, this will indicate China's willingness to pursue market-driven economic policies.
- India's ability to continue to reduce state intervention and encourage both national and international businesses to invest in its future.
- The strengthening of the ASEAN federation to give SE Asia greater cohesion.

■ The gap widens

The increasing gap between the rich and poor has the following implications for the world over the next 20 years:

- Increasing crime in the poorer parts of society will give rise to greater anxieties in the well-off sections of the community. Security is most women's greatest concern today in the West.
- Private security forces already outnumber state police in the US. We can expect this trend to increase. But who will police the police?
- Protection against theft, violence, and other forms of security provision for the individual will probably equal spending on health.

Continuing unabated this widening gap could result in anarchy.

■ Tribalism – ethnoscapes

The O.J. Simpson trial brought out the sharp divisions that exist between African Americans and their white fellow citizens. As previously with the Rodney King trial, this case divided largely along racial lines: 75 percent of black Americans thought that O.J. was not guilty, whilst an equivalent number of whites thought he was.

This raises some fundamental issues about the effectiveness of any judicial process. A jury, drawn from a cross-section of the community, is chosen from people who come to court already with deeply ingrained tribal beliefs based on the tribe or community they represent. John Katz, writing in *Wired* magazine, calls for a review of the existing judicial process: "Our society has no mechanism to try O.J. Simpson rationally. We can't deal with the debilitating social tensions of the case. And our legal process virtually guarantees that informed, fair-minded people be barred from juries."

> *O.J. raises some fundamental issues about the effectiveness of any judicial process.*

In 1963 when Martin Luther King led the civil rights march on Capitol Hill, both black and white Americans joined in the protest movement. In 1995, Louis Farrakhan, The Nation of Islam leader, led a march of 400,000 black-only men and called for total separation of black and white. His message was applauded by some white supremacists. "He is a man we can work with," said Mike Kemp, founder of the Gadsen Minutemen, a paramilitary group in Alabama.

O.J. Trial American Bar Association poll

Loss of faith in US judicial system

The anthropologist Arjun Appadurai has coined the word "ethnoscapes" to describe tribal communities which have their own complexity of values. What was America's melting pot earlier this century is turning into its "fruit salad." Marketeers will have much to learn from the need to meet the diverse needs of these groups.

> *What was America's melting pot earlier this century is turning into its "fruit salad."*

General Mills has tried to get around the problem by giving Betty Crocker, the icon of white middle America, a facelift. The new image on grocery products has been digitally "morphed" from 75 women of different races and ages. The company is trying what many other marketeers might be doing in future to market global products: seeking "ethnic diversity" in their brands – something which Coca-Cola has managed successfully for years.

Brainstorming the consequences

What are the eventual consequences if you take a two-tier theme to its logical conclusion? And not just inequality within a country, but regional and global inequality? What could be some of the counter forces?

Economist: It is not that clearly this will happen. If you look back over the last 150 years the absolute wealth of the world has increased by a factor of X or whatever. And there is an important distinction to be made between absolute and relative deprivation. There may well be two groups, but don't lose sight of the fact that these two groups are moving through time and space – the pull-through effect. In effect, if the rich get richer then the poor get less poor, although the gap in incomes might actually widen.

Also, there are other forces in the economy that will tend toward equilibrium. Consider the newly industrialized countries – since the Second World War, substantial blocs of the world have moved ahead in ways that few could have predicted 20 years ago.

> *Revolutions don't recur in truly repressed societies but in more open ones.*

Technologist: The Newly Industrialized Countries (NICs) have come up but the middle class in the US has come down in what could be called a pull-down effect – and this could be counter to an upward movement.

Sociologist: However, there is more permeability. There is a difference between a two-tier that is very solid and one which is permeable.

Marketeer: One thing to remember is that if you go back in time, there is a different expectation of wealth and living standards than there was 50 years ago. The raising of expectations also leads to more crime as people want what they see. Look at the LA riots, where people stole TV sets.

Sociologist Revolutions don't recur in truly repressed societies but in more open ones.

Politician: You could call it the revolution of rising expectations. What makes life difficult for politicians is that when you had rather different categories, with a relatively small percentage of people as middle class, you could base the system of two-party politics on that in a much more comfortable way. The haves and have-nots were more clearly defined. Now that statistics show that two-thirds of people have become much better off, and a third much worse off, you can't base a viable political party on a third of the population.

> *You can't base a viable political party on a third of the population.*

People are broadly better off. But is that plateauing? Halsey thought that 95 percent of people could be skilled to a high degree, but we don't raise them to that standard.

Sociologist: That is one of the countervailing forces to a two-tier society – training and education. The issue is whether in the last 40 years we have been living in what could be an historical aberration, and we go back to a situation where 10–15 percent will not have access to high skills and high-value-added training.

Marketeer: Who is going to pick a badly skilled American over a highly skilled Korean at half the price? People in the West have to realize the need for at least the minimum skills.

> *Who is going to pick a badly skilled American over a highly skilled Korean at half the price?*

Economist: There are many science fiction writers/films that portray a very bleak future in an industrialized world. And when you drive around the potholed streets of London, or try and get on the Metro in Paris or New York, it starts to hit you that what has happened in the industrialized world is that we have equipped ourselves with a huge infrastructure, capital goods that have to be maintained, and no one really gave it any thought about how they would keep it all going. And it is becoming immensely expensive. Look at all the Victorian sewers that have to be replaced in London, although they were built very well. But it is posing some real problems.

I take the view that when it comes to rich and poor it is a question of recycling – some groups do well and some badly. For the OECD countries, mastering the inheritance of the past – making sure we are up to speed in areas like education and social services provision – is quite a big issue. If they don't get it right, they will sink back into the second tier.

> *Some of the older cities and countries have just so much baggage.*

Sociologist: Some of the older cities and countries have just so much baggage.

Technologist: In London there is an enormous amount of old-style office accommodation which will never be used again as offices. So is it better to build new ones in London or move elsewhere?

Wealth keeping poverty out.

Author: If you go to a place like Rio you have the filthy rich and the filthy poor side by side, with rich corralled off. If you go to LA, you find another version of it. And then you drive to London's Hampstead Garden Suburb – it is on a smaller scale, but it is still wealth keeping poverty out.

Sociologist: The definition of poverty 150 years ago was defined by whether people had to work. That would cover 90 percent of people now. In between we have created a large bit in the middle. Whether that will happen in a place like Rio I'm not sure. But the pace of change has been swift in places like the UK.

Economist: The number of middle class in India is estimated to be 50–60 million. The question of whether you should be breaking the analysis down into countries or into smaller areas like cities allows you to get to grips better with the idea of tiers. Because even within a given country, there can be big differences.

Marketeer: There is also the question of the willingness to change. If you look at South America the top is still very corrupt. Corruption is still a very dangerous factor. Then there is the effect of TV. If you look at what happened in Poland, it went from being a repressed Third World country to a sophisticated market in a very short space of time.

Actor: It is the tension between the very upper and very lower tier that needs to be addressed.

Sociologist: Maybe it is a question of getting people to take a longer-term view. People used to think long term about their children's prospects – do they still do so?

Technologist: What is the definition of middle class? They have a bank account. They are more stable and life is more respected.

Politician: The number of people living in real poverty live day to day and are unskilled – can you break that? Are there examples of countries where that has been done? Japan, for example?

Technologist: Probably not Japan because the job market has been so artificial and so protected. A very large number of people work in small distribution companies and that can mop up an enormous number of unskilled people. Unemployment is now up to about 5.5 percent but has rarely been above 2.5 percent. Japan has however been more ruthless and systematic in their approach to education. They make sure people don't drop out.

Sociologist: Japan also has more protected sectors. If you think of some European countries, they have dropped out of many protected sectors as they have reengineered for globalization. One of my questions is do we recognize that there is a 20–30 percent at the bottom and conceive of ways of creating an economic structure that can accommodate them, or do we think that by education and training we can raise up most of them?

Technologist: But that 20 percent might become 80 percent within 30 years because you can make all the manufactured goods you want so easily that it might be a different mix of people but the same basic challenge: if you haven't got the impetus of a job every day, how do you make the whole thing work without harming global competitiveness?

Author: Who might over the next 20 years start to address the problems of the bottom 20 percent? Would it be governments, businesses, community? We have talked about what might happen but where will this countervailing force come from? Will major corporates around the world do it? It is said that western oil companies in Colombia make payments to people in outlying areas because they have pipelines on their land and the money no doubt helps keep them out of the clutches of the drug barons. It is a cost of doing business. And the government cannot do it because it doesn't have the resources.

> *If you haven't got the impetus of a job every day, how do you make the whole thing work?*

But then you have the Etzione idea that the community begins to act – there are a few US stories of people getting together to try and tackle the drugs problem. Who will be the initiators?

Marketeer: Sweden has put the emphasis on free education. Education gives people a chance to get out of the bottom layer and gives them hope.

Author: Latin cultures are very community-orientated but they are still poles apart in terms of rich and poor.

Technologist: Saving is not a very Latin thing.

Sociologist: It is interesting to look in America about why certain groups do or don't do well. For example, how come the Swedes and Germans did better in the US than the Irish and Italians at first? What about immigrants from Jamaica vs descendants of slaves?

Politician: Cornell did research that looked at Caribbean immigrants to the US and UK. The ones that went to the US this century are the second-most successful in terms of education and income after the Japanese, whereas in the UK they went to the bottom of the pile.

You can go a number of ways. You can do things like make cars impregnable with stronger security, etc., and have the richer guarding themselves. Or you can start looking at education, with areas like community service – even filling potholes – being used to give people a sense of work and achievement. All parties are looking at various forms of workfare.

Sociologist: If the kids at the bottom of the pile went to academies of crime we could teach them which ones weren't worth doing, like violent ones. It is much harder to catch fraudsters than car thieves.

Technologist: Corporate taxation could be used to encourage companies to do more in the communities. Perhaps give relief for helping small businesses. A lot of companies have done things like offering directors on secondment, but it is possible to speculate 10 years out – we could have the global 500 of the best corporate citizens. It will be a change of ethos because business has been so worried by the potential instability.

> **Corporate taxation could be used to encourage companies to do more in the communities.**

Sociologist: It is a way to deal with the fact that governments can't do some things very well. The trouble is, of course, the companies themselves are up against such massive change. But is there not a cost for not doing it? Because otherwise insecurity can increase.

Author: What will banks be doing to address the two-tier gap? What about the rise of credit unions in rundown inner city areas?

Economist: My gut feeling is that banks will continue to provide service to those with money. Anyway, because of the regulatory structure, banks tend to react, not push things. Banks are huge vacuum cleaners for savings. So they centralize the money and try and do something with it. The issue for banks is how can they be involved in more creative relationships with areas they haven't been in before, like venture capital to allow them to throw a bit more seedcorn and generate higher income later. But I am not convinced this is something banks can do well.

> **Banks are huge vacuum cleaners for savings.**

Marketeer: What about microlending as in Indian villages? It works on the village principle, where if one person defaults, the village suffers.

Politician: That is how working class skilled people founded what are building societies in the UK and mutuals in the US. All those social banks have disappeared. Will they be reinvented?

Sociologist: What were social banks have become institutionalized and centralized away from where they began.

Author: Bartering is also being seen more. There are some experiments in local currency where people build up credits. It's so many units for plastering your wall, so much for wiring the house, or fixing your car.

Politician: In the Networking for Industry program, one group is doing a community audit in a deprived area and a village, and seeing what skills are there. Then you use new technology and build up a database for skills swapping. You can also begin to ask people what skills they want.

Economist: There is scope if the government or local government feels there is a service needed. There could be a joint initiative between banks, industry, and government to redirect flows of money in the directions it wouldn't go in, left to themselves. But that runs into the problem of organizing and planning and you can end up with white elephants if you are not careful.

The vectors of change – economics

Resourcing the world

The future for the world's resources is of interest to the many energy companies, the utilities and also to the suppliers of food and raw materials. Shortages of certain resources also indicates the potential for conflict in areas of the world and would undoubtedly imply rising prices. Equally the potential for finding ample supply of key raw materials or energy would lead to good times for local economies as evidenced in the last two decades by Norway, Alaska and Scotland's Grampian region. We discuss below the prospects for world resources and in particular how China may cope with sustaining its expanding economy.

Highlights

- *China's appetite*
- *Water – the oil of the 21st century*
- *Fossil fuels*

If China's per capita consumption of fish equalled that of Japan, they would consume the entire world's fish stocks in one year.

■ China's appetite, the world's wake-up call

Worldwatch Institute, a US-based organization, has examined some of the eventual resource implications on the world's resources if China continues its economic growth unabated:

- By 2030 China will need to import 200 million tons of grain, all of the world's current production.
- If every Chinese person had one egg a day it is estimated that the 1.3 billion hens in 2000 will require more grain to feed than the entire annual output of Australia.
- If the Chinese appetite for fish equals the per capita consumption of Japan's, then it alone will consume the entire world's fish harvest of 100 million tons.

In 1995 China was 162 in the World Bank ranking of national wealth and natural resources. Although the country may soon become the largest economy in the world, it will rely on a significant volume of trade in order to meet its growing appetite for food, energy, and raw materials.

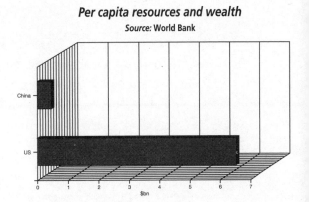

Per capita resources and wealth
Source: World Bank

■ Water – the oil of the 21st century

Approximately 1 percent of the world's water, if available for drinking, would normally be sufficient to satisfy the needs of the planet. However, all the available water is not evenly distributed and in many parts of Africa, India, and the Middle East people suffer from chronic water shortages leading to the need to divert or redirect rivers and tap into ancient aquifers. In many instances this interferes with the flow of rivers which may pass more than one country and has given rise to war and conflict. Water wars are most likely in the Middle East, where Jordan's river by the same name has been diverted by Israel and where Egypt's famous life-giving river, the Nile, is dependent on upstream Sudan. Meanwhile, Turkey is busy with building dams on the Euphrates, which affects Syria and Iraq downstream.

Scientists and hydrologists are both agreed that the future direction to resolving the water crisis in the world's driest regions comes from conservation and efficient use of the existing water supplies. Leakage and evaporation are the two main culprits of water loss and the Israelis have long since mastered the art of drip-feed irrigation to improve the usability of water.

Leakage is up to 50 percent in many cities and transmission systems in both the developed and undeveloped world. There were calls for the resignation of the Chief Executive of one water company in the UK where, during a prolonged drought, it was revealed that the company's transmission pipes leaked away half the water they transported.

Water taxation will become a new form of revenue for governments and we should expect different grades of water with varying purity standards; for drinking, washing or industrial uses.

Breakthrough in the creation of antimatter

Early in 1996 scientists at CERN in Switzerland announced that they had created nine atoms of antimatter, an achievement which was hailed by the scientific community as one of the most significant technical breakthroughs since the development of the atom bomb. A solitary atom of antimatter has the potential to release huge amounts of energy and could pave the way for cheap, pollution-free energy.

■ Fossil-based fuels

These have been the mainstay of fuel provision throughout this century and should continue to maintain that position for much of the next 20 years. Demands for fossil fuel in the developed world are likely to be static as any small incremental usage from economic growth is compensated for by greater conservation. It is in the developing economies of Asia that the demands for fuel will be most prevalent.

Alternative sources of energy such as renewable sources and new breakthroughs in fuel cell technology will take some time to permeate through to large-scale mainstream usage within the time horizons of our look at the future. Unless there are new discoveries in non-fossil energy sources, the world could begin to face fuel shortages towards the end of the second decade, next century.

Brainstorming the consequences

Author: China will be the world's biggest economy in ten years' time. The implication: if every Chinese person had one egg a day, there would need to be 1.2 billion eggs is mind boggling.

Sociologist: Biotechnology/agricultural technology could solve this problem, if we ran out of food.

Economist: China is huge but the system will adjust. It always has in the past. Also, agriculture has been characterized by surplus.

Marketeer: Packaging could be improved so food could be transported without being destroyed. Up to 90 percent of food can be destroyed in transit to some places like Russia. Distribution, not food, is the issue.

Strategist: There are still quite a lot of companies who are investing in Africa. While that continues then we have some hope for that continent's resource shortfall.

> *Up to 90 percent of food can be destroyed in transit.*

Sociologist: Maybe the way to solve Africa's problems is to divide it up into portions and solve it bit by bit.

Politician: Hamish MacRae, the journalist and author, is very pessimistic about South Africa – he thinks the whites will leave.

Technologist: To be able to get a reasonable living standard you have to get the birth rate down and educational standards up. The more people, the less education, the less money to spread around. IT could help with communication, with remote learning and work through infusion on getting the birth rate down.

> *To be able to get a reasonable living standard you have to get the birth rate down.*

Strategist: Why is the developed world interested in Africa? The cynical view is that you must invest in Africa, stabilize it, educate it – why? Otherwise there will be mass movements of population to Europe, which it can't afford. There is also the fear that a lot of incurable and less understood viruses originate in Africa. These could spread like wildfire unless controlled.

Economist: The point is that Africa has a lot of natural resources – minerals, etc. – but it is harder to get them out now because since decolonization many countries are unstable – civil war in Angola, for example.

Sociologist: The biggest natural resource problem is water – less than 1 percent of the available water in the southern hemisphere is available to Africa.

Author: But how about China – it's estimated there will be 600 million boys – will they be spoiled brats? (Girls are abandoned to a large extent.) It could be the little emperor syndrome – all these families with one child. What are the implications? Will these children know how to share?

Technologist: When you get a surplus of men you get wars.

> *When you get a surplus of men you get wars.*

Economist: There are 300 million bank accounts in China already.

Sociologist: There are inheritance implications if the inheritance is coming to one person. Some economists believe in the gradual diminution of the US as a global power. But that could be too early – anything could happen in China.

Author: What services will these 600 million children want? Do they want what all kids want? Do they buy into the global thing?

Economist: Remember China also has the problem of dealing with an ageing population. An issue will be the family transfer of resources – what if all of them are gobbled up by care for the aged? Will there be a push for family or non-family scenario? Possibly the elderly do not want the family scenario because there will be more responsibility than joy in taking care of grandchildren.

The vectors of change – social

Post-consumerism

Post-consumerism is a vector which defines the new customer culture we are entering as we leave behind several decades of "conspicuous" consumption. In the developed world customers have reached saturation point in consumer durables, electronic gadgetry, automobiles and so on. Companies like Procter & Gamble, who have been the leading proponents of modern marketing, slashed their advertising budgets in 1996 by $1.6 billion in an effort to respond to price competition. What are the attitudes and values of the new generation of consumers? These will become harder to understand and anticipating them will be key to the success of most companies in the years to come. We explore some of these attitudes where they have already become evident.

Highlights

- *Efficient societies*
- *Quality of life*
- *Generation X*
- *Calvin Klein turns on Xers*
- *Solitaries*
- *Buddhism booms*

- *Vegetarianism*
- *Overweight and obesity*
- *Drugs*
- *Kids up-age looks*
- *Gambling takes off*
- *No older role models*

■ Efficient societies

The efficiency of a society as measured by factors such as low crime rates, close family units, good educational attainment, and access to good healthcare will be increasingly sought after by countries and will be assessed in parallel with economic statistics.

In Aldous Huxley's *Brave New World* the United States of the World's motto declares, "community, identity and stability." Not very far from the virtues espoused by the state of Singapore. Although many Westerners could not accept social conditioning, the way Singapore has managed its way through to become not only the most successful economy over the last 25 years but to also score highly on most of the measures quoted above. In the 1970s, shortly after the end of British rule, the GDP per head was below $1,000. Today the figure is 13 times higher, rivalling that of many developed countries. Unlike Japan, Singapore is culturally diverse, with Chinese, Malayans, Indians, and Europeans sharing in the economic prosperity of the country. It has no natural resources, even its water is piped in from Malaysia.

Singapore's social problems are few by Western standards, the educational achievement of its pupils is amongst the highest in the world, and most citizens have access to primary healthcare. The state is now engaged in an active program of trying to assert traditional Asian family values on its citizens to arrest the gradual increase in divorce rates and to cope with the increase in its ageing population. Marriage, procreation, and respect and care of parents are being promoted. Social engineering includes ensuring that educated single women find partners to marry by providing a state-run dating service. Single mothers also find it more difficult to buy government accommodation and there are tax disincentives for employing maids and other home help. Parents also have a right since 1994 to sue their children for maintenance payments.

Are countries like Singapore a model which countries or communities might emulate in the future?

Are countries like Singapore a model which countries or communities might emulate in the future? Citizens or members of a community who do not wish to play by the rules set down are not welcome. Everybody knows the rules and plays by them because they can visibly see the benefits. Singaporeans may not like some of the authoritarian dictats of Lee Kuan Yew, but not many would feel motivated to bring change to their system as long as it works.

■ Quality of life

In the developed world, the quality of life or living standards will increasingly become a source of measurement rather than traditional statistics of GNP growth. France, say, with a GNP per head of $20,000 does not seem 50 times richer than India, with a GNP per head of $400. Many activities in the Indian economy would not be measured as in France. When a Parisian couple both go out to work they would employ a nanny or childminder to look after their children. In Bombay a mother would remain in the home to look after the children, or the services of the grandparents in the extended family may be employed in the business of child rearing. The French childminder's role is measured in the economy whilst the Indian one isn't.

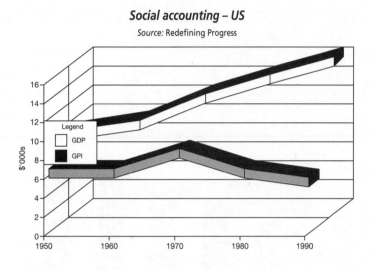

Social accounting – US

Source: Redefining Progress

The United States is an example where existing economic measures do not reflect the living standards of a country. Although GNP has risen by 30 percent over the last 20 years, arguably living standards have not. Many may feel they have actually declined.

> *A majority of people felt that in exchange for extra time at home they would be prepared to forfeit up to 20 percent of their earnings.*

Redefining Progress, a green US think tank based in San Francisco, has redefined traditional economics by publishing its own "genuine progress indicator" (GPI). The GPI captures such items as housework and the volunteer sector. They subtract from GDP figures, costs associated with crime, and depletion of natural resources. The model of social accounting shows the growing gap between traditional GDP and the GPI, in the think tank's view the true long-term state of the economy.

In a survey in the US when people were asked how much they would give up for an extra day a week with their family, a majority of people felt that in exchange for extra time at home they would be prepared to forfeit up to 20 percent of their earnings. For the first time since the Second World War, young people are begining to feel that they will not be able to exceed the living standards of their parents. A UK study showed that only 40 percent of 16–24-year-olds felt that their living standards would be better than those of their parents. Other age groups continue to be optimistic about the future.

■ Generation X

Generation X, the post-baby boom generation, has been researched extensively in the United States to develop a profile of the type of customers who may be at the peak of spending power within the next decade. Clear differences between the two generations are evident, many of which cannot be explained by age differences alone. Xers have been given responsibility earlier, they have matured earlier, and many have had sexual relationships five or six years earlier than their parents although electing to stay single for longer. They are overall less well off than their parents and spend their scarce resources less frequently but on extravagances for themselves.

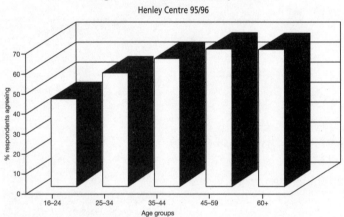

Living standards better than parents

Henley Centre 95/96

By the age of 20 Xers had watched nearly 24,000 hours of television, several thousand hours of advertising, and have become skeptical about any claim made by advertisers. This makes them very sophisticated and discerning customers. Manufacturers have to be careful not to underestimate the intelligence of Xers or exaggerate the features of their products. Xers will therefore only buy something when they can touch, feel, see, and try out the goods on offer.

Many have had sexual relationships five or six years earlier than their parents.

Their value-consciousness extends beyond the products they sell to the way suppliers run their organizations. The ethical stance of Anita Roddick's Body Shop, which retails personal products, helps sell the natural body and skin care toiletries. Timberland's campaigns on racism and urban regeneration help sell its no-nonsense, hardwearing clothing and footwear. Ben and Jerry's egalitarian employment practices played well to the pure, unadulterated ice cream in an age of additive-ridden mass-produced foods. Virgin Airlines boss

Richard Branson's high-profile support for environmental issues has positioned the brand well with Xers. MTV employs Xers to run the channel, thereby helping management better understand their audience. In contrast, when Coca-Cola launched "Fruitopia," the $30 million campaign produced an initial jump in sales but fell back disappointingly within a year. Consumers didn't feel that Coca-Cola's "Fruitopia: for the mind, body and planet" campaign was genuine, nor did it fit well with the mass market, megacorpo-

By the age of 20 Xers have watched nearly 24,000 hours of television.

rate image of this giant corporation. In contrast, they were, and continue to be, quite happy drinking Classic Coke.

Xers enjoy shopping, spend more time doing it than boomers, admit to doing it mainly for emotional reasons, and are more demanding in the customer service they expect from retailers. Their requirements for service extend to knowledgable salespeople, stylish shop layouts, and quick service when they have made their choice. US shopping malls have begun to offer a range of add-on

> **Xers enjoy shopping.**

entertainment to attract customers. Electronic games arcades, multiplex cinemas, skating rinks and live theater have been used to make shopping entertaining.

In keeping with their personal relationships, Xers are less loyal to brands. They will not hesitate to switch brands if a competitor offers better quality and value. The ability for, or even the illusion of, beating the system implies value to many. Some will take great pleasure in telling friends that they know the cheapest place in town to buy a pair of Levi's, irrespective of the journey-time and cost to get there. This extends to their viewing habits as they "surf" through a hundred or more

> **The ability for, or even the illusion of, beating the system implies value to many.**

channels looking for a program they like. Many admit to watching more than one program at the same time, switching between the "boring" bits. This represents a challenge to the advertisers, who are unable to pinpoint a typical viewing audience with a specific channel.

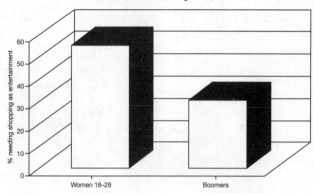

Shopping as entertainment

Source: Mademoiselle Magazine (US)

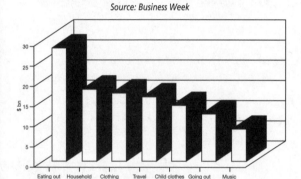

18–29-year-olds' – purchases (1991–US)

Source: Business Week

Xers believe in the importance of expressing their individuality and resist attempts to stereotype them. This probably emphasizes the growing importance of one-to-one marketing.

A UK survey of 18–34-year-olds by Socioconsult concluded the following:

- This is the most educated generation ever, women having nearly twice the qualifications of the older generations.
- They have a fragmented set of "post material" values associated with autonomy and authenticity, meaning rather than status.
- Men's values become more feminine and women's values become more masculine.
- Four times the number of younger Xers are in temporary employment than any other age group.
- 20 percent of women earn more than their male counterparts, up from 7 percent 10 years ago.

■ Calvin Klein turns on Xers

In the 1995 campaign for the perfume "cK one," launched around the world by Calvin Klein, the slogan "as sexy as the truth" was used to promote the

> **This is the most educated generation ever, women having nearly twice the qualifications of the older generations.**

product. Its posters depicted a group of men and women, in the 20–30 age band, represented from all five continents and clad in a self-consciously inelegant style. Its screw-top bottle and retailing through popular outlets such as record stores were accompanied by a high-powered media campaign usually reserved for more upmarket and high margin perfumes. According to industry analysts the perfume has been highly success-ful, having targeted a group of cus-tomers who don't go near any of the specialist perfume boutiques and yet have the willingness to spend on luxury items.

■ Solitaries

A new breed of 25–35-year-old is emerging, best described as the soli-taries. They would probably work for a software house, a media business, or an investment bank and spend 14 hours a day at the office. Their most fre-quent food is a cook-chill supper for one, bought at about 8.30pm and con-sumed an hour later in front of the TV in their stylish warehouse-riverside

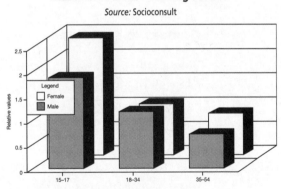

Masculine values – crude hedonism
Source: *Socioconsult*

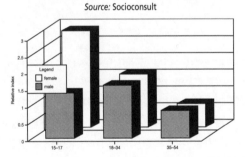

Masculine values – risk taking
Source: Socioconsult

Masculine values – seeking success
Source: Socioconsult

appartment furnished with flair. They are more private and less sociable than their peers of similar age, highly discriminating, and verge on the austere in their dress code. When they buy presents, it's usually a treat for themselves: a $100 tie from Milan, a $3,000 antique pinball machine for the apartment. Loneliness is their greatest fear, how-ever they work hard at disguising it by the active life they lead. Political correctness in the office makes it difficult to form relationships and they would resort to introduction agencies to meet a partner. The quality of this growing and often unscrupu-lous service sector falls well short of expectations for the solitary. Singapore has introduced a government dating service to specifically cater for this sector.

> *When they buy presents, it's usually a treat for themselves.*

If they do marry for the first time it will be no earlier than 28 for a man and 26 for a woman.

> **WHAT THE SOLITARY EATS**
> - Takeaways, usually the more eclectic the better
> - Tit-bits such as pizza slices, treacle pudding, Stollen
> - Instant, cook-chill dishes and TV dinners purchased late
>
> **WHAT THE SOLITARY READS**
> - Two or three newspapers, at least one junk version
> - Lifestyle magazines
> - Airport bookstand bestsellers
>
> **WHERE THE SOLITARY HOLIDAYS**
> - Singles usually in the Carribean
> - Walking in Nepal
> - Sailing, with a club, in the Med

Owners to custodians

With a future of low inflation and slow growth rates, customers are likely to take to hiring or leasing as a means of protection against loss in value of capital purchases and of obsolescence. The car you purchase is worth 20 percent less the day you drive it out of the showroom, the PC you buy is becoming obsolete as you unpack it. One car dealer summed it up, "People buying a car with their own hard-earned capital are crazy these days. Not a week goes by without someone announcing a deal that's better than the one we heard about last week. Why should I buy a car when I can trade it in for a guaranteed buy back price in a year?" The Ford for Life campaign and Mercedes' plan for a car-for-all-seasons are all directed at encouraging people to be custodians rather than owners.

The mind-body connection

Old ailments are being understood in new ways and powerful new treatments are emerging today as medical researchers exploit rapidly emerging knowledge about the nature of the human genome and the reversibility of biochemical reactions in the body. Dr Frank Wetzel, a New Jersey psychotherapist, says that conditions such as depression, anxiety and certain personality problems are now treated with a combination of psychotropic drugs and talk therapy. Many psychiatric conditions such as manic-depressive illness and schizophrenia, which are costly to manage, are now considered to have substantial genetic components. Previously intractable symptoms of psychological trauma can now be treated in many cases by variants of cognitive-behavior therapy, with or without the assistance of drugs. Michael Douglas, the Hollywood actor, was reported to have taken treatment from a clinic for sexual addiction and thousands of people every day attend clinics or self-help groups for a range of other addictions including gambling, overspending, alcoholism, drug abuse, eating disorders, and "relationship hunger."

Wetzel also points out that advances in tracking the biochemistry of the brain in recent years has led to several new generations of antidepressants and antipsychotic drugs which seek to correct "chemical imbalances" in the brain. They are more likely to be used in tandem with one-to-one counselling and group programs than ever before, which has led to greater regulation of therapists' activities. "Talk therapy alone has its place, but adjunctive treatment with powerful drugs is already becoming the norm," says Wetzel. "Prozac," a drug to treat depression, has become a household name, and in some circles "He's on Prozac," is commonly used as a sarcastic description of some high performing individual.

■ Buddhism booms

What do Richard Gere, Koo Stark, Harrison Ford, John Cleese, Philip Glass, and Tina Turner have in common? The answer is they have all sought refuge in Buddhism to escape from the day-to-day traumas of Western-styled living. Buddhism is booming in the West according to the various centers which have sprung up in Europe and North America. People seem to be attracted to the religion because of its intellectual

Buddhism is booming in the West.

approach. A devotee was reported in *The Guardian* newspaper as saying, "Usually if you get into mysticism everything starts turning vague, in any tradition. That is for me what appealed: I don't have to dump my intellect to do something with spirituality."

■ Vegetarianism

The meat content in people's diets has moved from ideology to concern about the implications for healthy living. Heart disease, overweight, and a variety of bacteriological diseases have been associated with excessive meat consumption. "Mad cow disease" in cattle has substantially reduced the consumption of beef in Germany, and periodic publicity over factory farming techniques has depressed consumers' appetite for meat in many markets. A UK Gallup survey showed that over 7 percent of people avoided red meat compared with 2 percent a year ago. Restaurants and catering establishments in most international cities are beginning to offer vegetarian options on their menus. Meat producers have responded with advertising campaigns extolling the virtues of meat in an attempt to lift flagging sales.

Those avoiding red meat

Source: UK Gallup survey

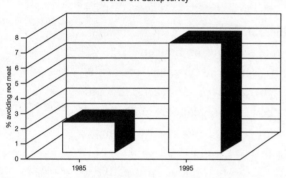

■ Overweight and obesity

The incidence of overweight people and their vulnerability to diabetes, heart disease, and strokes have prompted the trend towards healthy, low-fat foods and exercise. However, thanks to the increase in the snacking culture of essentially unhealthy foods, the percentage of overweight people has continued to increase in many countries. It is estimated that more than 50 percent of British people are overweight according to the Department of Health, with men suffering marginally more from this condition than women.

Procter & Gamble have obtained FDA approval for the first zero calorie fat product which will probably do for food what Nutrasweet did for soft drinks. Although it has the same consistency as ordinary fat, it doesn't have the calories. The product "Olean" is composed of large enough molecules so that it is not absorbed as it makes its way through the digestive system. Potato chips fried in normal fat are about 150 calories an ounce. Fried in Olean, it's less than 60 calories. One existing drawback is that the substance can have a laxative effect if taken in quantity and the initial approval by the FDA is only for salted snacks such as corn chips and P&G's winning snack, Pringles.

But low fat foods are not universally accepted by customers. In the US, McDonald's withdrew their low fat hamburgers after a spell of four unsuccessful years of trying to promote their McLean Delux range. The customers who pop into the company's food outlets seem to prefer a "hearty" meal with all the trimmings, which has helped to make North America's population one of the most obese on earth.

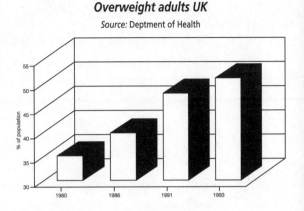

Overweight adults UK
Source: Deptment of Health

The growth of "functional foods" such as Benecol's cholesterol reducing margarine, fruit drinks with soluble fiber from SmithKline Beecham and vitamin-containing yoghurts has been finding great success in the market. This trend should increase for the health-conscious consumer.

■ 30 million haven't inhaled

It is estimated that 30 million Americans have taken marijuana at some time. Studies have shown that 13 percent of 14-year-olds have tried the weed, up from 6 percent three years ago. Marijuana is classed as a Schedule I drug, which puts it in the same category as harder drugs such as LSD and heroin There have been various calls to legalize marijuana, most notably by Joycelyn Elders, the US Surgeon General, and both President

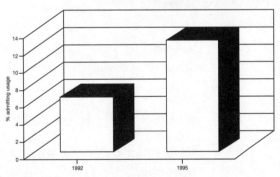

Marijuana users – 14 years of age
Source: University of Michigan

Clinton and Speaker Gingrich have admitted to smoking pot at some time in the past. The drug is used unofficially by many suffering from AIDS and cancer.

There have frequently been calls to legalize the drug or downgrade its classification. Proponents of legalization argue that marijuana is less harmful than tobacco and that legalization would drive out of business the various crime syndicates that deal in the drug.

Amsterdam has an unofficial policy of turning a blind eye to the trade in pot in its bars and cafés. The policy has been in operation since the 1960s and only recently have there been calls to clamp down on the drug's use in public.

■ Kids up-age looks

In the blockbuster teenage movie *Clueless* the two main characters, Alicia and Cher, are both 15 but dress to be older than their years. One babyboomer describes the current state of teen fashion as conservative, dull, and boring. "When I was a teenager the last thing I wanted was to look 30."

■ Gambling takes off

Publicity surrounding the launch of the National Lottery in Britain in 1994 reached fever pitch for most of the year as mostly lower-income hopefuls and the elderly sought a chance to become millionaires overnight. The Hollywood movie *It Could Happen to You*, the story of a New York policeman and a waitress winning the jackpot, was a hit with people who had caught lottery fever.

Meanwhile back in the US, where $500 billion is bet legally every year making gambling an estimated $40 billion industry, virtual casinos were beginning to emerge, giving the industry the opportunity to explode. Currently most states forbid the practice of gambling when it crosses national or state borders. However, entrepreneurial businesses have begun offering betting services on the Internet from offshore companies in the Caribbean and so far appear to be getting away with it. Gambling offers the underworld the opportunity to launder the billions of illegal drug dollars that are generated every year.

> Meanwhile back in the US, where $500 billion is bet legally every year . . .

■ Lack of older role models

In the considerably younger developing world, young people will not have an older population to look up to and help them formulate their ideas and aspirations for the future. They will therefore increasingly take their cues from their peer group, who will in turn be influenced by Western-styled media and television beamed from satellites around the world.

These are some of the implications of a younger world:

- Areas of the world with disaffected youth will be subject to great instability.
- Mass markets could be created, aimed at a global youth cult.

There may emerge a Maoist-type figure to channel the energies of the young. This would be unlikely to happen in China, which is a population that has already begun to age, or in Europe. Africa or South America are perfect candidates for such a revolution.

Brainstorming the consequences

Politician: The Western world has been stable over the last 20 years. There was the "milk" round for students where students were courted by employers. All that has disappeared. This is true across the Western world.

Marketeer: It is a question now of finding your place in the scheme of things, something you are interested in. Children are more instantly aware of what's in and what isn't. Also, they have grown up with media as primary input. This will affect society greatly 30 years on. But how?

> **Children are more instantly aware of what's in and what isn't.**

Author: What will we be watching in ten years' time? What sort of issues will we be dealing with?

Actor: I think there will still be a desire for quality from the higher tier. Quality? Historical drama, Shakespeare. That will be one strand. There will also be a lowest common denominator: game shows, high-action speed drama. It is getting cheaper to make with special effects. Hollywood spectaculars will come to TV. But there is still a middle section who want to see news documentaries, etc.

Economist: What about international TV? There is still a problem with language. (Although it does have a technical solution because Germans, for example, can offer dubbed and non-dubbed films.) But there will be more internationalization in areas like sport.

Sociologist: It could widen the price range. So you will pay more for higher quality. What are the implications for the lower tier? There could be increasing divergence.

Marketeer: One of the problems for expensive programs is that program makers are not sure they will find enough of a market. With globalization they will find that critical market – like *Brideshead Revisited* and *Inspector Morse*. All have made millions around the world.

> **Those without work have nothing to do during the day but watch TV.**

Politician: There was an argument that social cohesion in countries was helped because most people saw the same program at the same time. It created a sense of community.

> *All the political parties are looking at this – in the sense of creating community armies.*

What about those without work who have nothing to do during the day but watch TV?

Technologist: Is there a way to use the media, technology, to provide more access to role models and aspirations? What tools have we got to get that mindset? Colin Powell was drafted into the army and has been a source of inspiration to minorities. Maybe we should draft citizens into people armies.

> *Fundamental Islam? Is it a harkening back to tried and true values?*

Politician: All the political parties are looking at this – in the sense of creating community armies.

Technologist: It is also a way of taking people out of their environment.

Politician: A lot of the kids in the underclass in the US never move off the block. In my area many of the younger people will never go to London. But they see all these attractions on films, TV.

Economist: If the pace of change accelerates and people are discomforted by it and get a perception that things are not improving, is there not a risk that people will put their foot down? For example, what about the resurgence of fundamental Islam? Is it a hearkening back to tried and true values? A way to control?

Sociologist: There is an intolerance in fundamentalism but some of it is inner-directed. For example, some Turkish Muslim women want to wear the veil.

Economist: The problem is that our society believes that things continue to get better – the Victorian idea of progress.

Author: Some pundits are saying it is the end of consumerism. Look at New Age travelers – they are the hippies of the 1990s. There are more groups like that. Society is seen as all too complex. People are opting out of careers at 50–55 from the growth thing.

Technologist: There is a lot more in terms of goods, but in terms of disposable incomes people will not feel richer than their parents.

Author: Accountants invented the P&L, the balance sheet, but have we reached the point where accounts also need to take an holistic view? If I am a long-term shareholder, I want to know not so much if the company will survive the next quarter, but in 15 years' time because my pension might depend on it. So is there a parallel form of measures that takes a wider view?

Technologist: We have moved more to companies built on concepts, with franchises, etc. But banks still look at tangible assets. How do you measure intangibles? In France a chef can get funding according to their Michelin rating.

In France a chef can get funding according to their Michelin rating.

Author: At NASDAQ the information in the prospectus is often based on forecasts of future worth. Now it has a market capitalization nearly as big as the NYSE. This has taken place over the last 10–15 years. There are a lot of positive things we are not picking up that are off the radar screen. Beta factors are a similar concept – a quasi-quantitative factor. Netscape, with $50K/quarter sales, went on to NASDAQ for millions. Maybe Europe needs a NASDAQ? After all, the UK-equivalent Unipalm didn't go on to the London Stock Exchange.

Technologist: There are two possible influences for consumers. One is that Europe gets more and more influenced by North American attitudes and style and we all end up behaving like Americans. The other is that because of the rising consumer markets in Asia, Europe is more influenced by those areas.

The vectors of change – social

The end of patriarchy

Births to unmarried mothers

Source: The Economist/Senator Moynihan

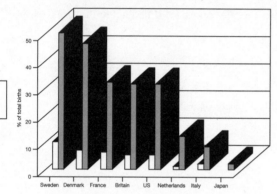

The structure of the family determines some of the fundamental ways in which we live and bring up the new generation of citizens. The traditional post-industrial nuclear family is changing in the Western world to one which is more fragmented, increasingly based on single parent relationships or just single unmarried men and women. This puts new demands on housing, employment and child care. Both private and state-run organizations serving parents and families need to be aware of these changes and be prepared to respond accordingly. In this chapter we deal with some of the changes that have been taking place in the family and consider some of the countervailing forces which might resist change.

Highlights

- *Marriage, a changing contract*
- *Older parents*
- *East vs West values*

■ Marriage, a changing contract

Over the last 20 years the structure of the family has been changing. Partnership and parenthood are being decoupled and women have found it feasible to raise children without men. These are some of the significant changes we have seen:

- The married couple living with their own children is becoming a minority. Less than 20 percent of families correspond to this model in many cities of the developed world.
- Fewer than 30 percent of adolescents will have lived together with their mother and father by the time they are adults.
- Single parent/mother families have reached as high as 60 percent in some US cities and are running at around 30 percent in most major cities in the Western world.
- More children are being born out of marriage. In Britain, France, and the US, around 30 percent of children are born to unmarried parents, up from 6 percent in 1960.
- The divorce rate has doubled in many Western countries in the last 20 years. Although divorce in Asia is low, in countries like Singapore the rate has been steadily rising to a current one in seven marriages.
- Single parent or broken homes are frequently at the bottom of the economic ladder with nearly three quarters of these households needing income support in the UK.

Society has not been able to adapt to these changes in the structure of the family, and many of the dysfunctional problems, particularly in males, can be traced back to the lack of a mother and father in a family relationship. Research has shown that children from broken homes have greater difficulties at school, keeping relationships themselves, and keeping a job. Boys without fathers are more prone to casual sex and violence, and girls are more likely to be young unmarried mothers.

The breakup of the family structure is a drain on the economies where this is highest. Frequently the state has to support the children and one of the parents. In some cases this support is insufficient, the children suffer, the likelihood of them taking to crime increases, and soon we are in a spiral towards social breakdown. It also is a drain on the economy as the money devoted to fighting crime and supporting marital breakdown could be channeled elsewhere.

The increase in one-parent households has increased throughout the Western world, with the greatest numbers being in Northern Europe and the US. These are some of the motivations which would increase state intervention in preventing marital breakdown in the future. They will come in the form of both economic sanctions and compulsory reconciliation periods. It is arguable if any of these measures will have an effect on the overall trend.

> **The traditional nuclear family may soon be in a minority.**

An inter-departmental working group has been set up by the UK government to develop the most radical reform of the divorce laws in the last 25 years. Ending the "quickie divorce" and replacing it with a 12-month cooling-off period has been considered. This is after the UK Office of Population Censuses and Surveys announced that marriages had fallen to their lowest level for the last 50 years.

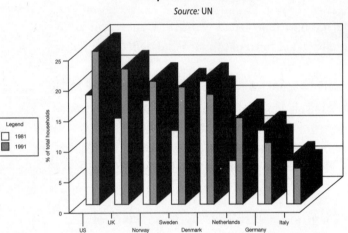

One parent households
Source: UN

Germany has used a range of taxation, benefit, and legal measures to keep the family unit intact. Married couples pay less tax, children reduce the tax burden even further, mothers have their jobs protected for up to three years after birth, and there are incentives for keeping dependants. In Sweden marriage is not rewarded through taxation or any significant benefits from the state. People are taxed as individuals. Whilst many more women go out to work and have a good deal of independence, divorce in Sweden is three times that in Germany.

Although governments have been trying to protect the trend in the breakup of the family, there are some who believe that this institution is due for a change. Sheila McKechnie, once head of Shelter, a UK charity for the homeless and now Chief Executive of the Consumer's Association, voices her views on behalf of many feminists. "The family as we have known it has been a source of oppression to many women and we should not underestimate the effect it has had."

In certain sectors women are finding it easier to gain employment than men and we are beginning to see a form of role reversal. Working class men in the

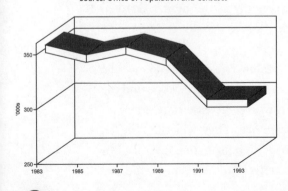

UK marriages 1983–93
Source: Office of Population and Censuses

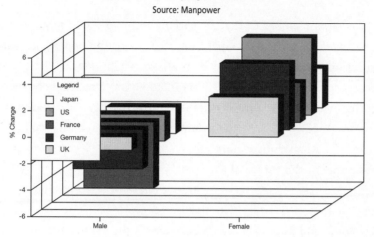

Male/Female employment 1981–94

Source: Manpower

North of England are staying at home while their wives or girlfriends go to work in factories, offices, or catering establishments.

Experts in family therapy are putting forward the idea that marriage may in fact be changing from a type of contract between two individuals to a continuous unspoken negotiation. The two parties may in fact regularly re-evaluate their position in the relationship as their circumstances and preferences change.

The generation X opinion data suggests a similar ethos regarding customer relationships. Consumers are only prepared to repeatedly purchase goods and services provided suppliers can repeatedly demonstrate quality, value, and whatever else might be the stated attributes. Traditional customer loyalty as we have known it may be an unattainable ideal in the future, being replaced by an ongoing negotiation between supplier and customer.

■ Older parents

Parents are marrying later in life and having children later than their counterparts ten years earlier. The UK average age for marriage for males in 1995 was 28 years of age and 26 for women, up from 25 and 23 ten years earlier. A similar trend is to be observed elsewhere in the developed world.

> *Marriage is changing from a contract to a continuous negotiation between two individuals.*

East vs West values

David Howell, a member of the UK parliament, in a 1995 newspaper article for the *Independent* newspaper entitled "Europe must prepare for Easternization," called for the need to adopt Asian values. The probability that Asian capitalism will come to dominate global markets is borne out by the fact that with fast-growing economies in the region, their traditional high savings rates (Japan's 56 percent vs the US's 5 percent), greater value attached to education, and a stronger family-based culture the West may have to take on board some of the values of the East.

Already Japanese management techniques have been adopted in most manufacturing companies. The Confucian ideology of minimal distinction between work and play is in sharp contrast to the Western thinking of "all work and no play makes Jack a dull boy." The yin and yang Chinese philosophy of "you lose by gaining and you gain by losing" is difficult to come to terms with in a Western world of "black and white" thinking. Equally at odds with Western business ethics is the apparently open *"baksheesh"* mentality of Asian cultures where sometimes people unrelated to a particular contract award or purchase require hand-outs before a deal can be concluded.

So far the West, from its economically powerful position, has been able to call on the rest of the world to adopt its values for successful organization. When purchasing power is more balanced between East and West it is likely that we may see a greater cross-fertilization of values. Asian leaders have been keen to point out to Western commentators and critics that their success is down to hard work and social values. Malaysia's prime minister, Dr Mahathir Mohamad, and Singapore's Lee Kuan Yew are known to have been most vocal in this area.

Brainstorming the consequences

One argument says get back to traditional values. Another is that we need to find a new way to organize. The third is a vicious spiral of one-parent families producing one-parent families: perpetuating the poverty trap.

Sociologist: Why is the family so stressed? At the heart of it is women's liberation based on the pill, the control of reproduction. Women also have more economic power through more education. And morality has changed – before, morality was based on preventing unwanted pregnancies.

Technologist: The best way of decreasing family size in developing countries is to increase education. So we have much smaller families in the developed world and increasingly in the underdeveloped countries. When families were big, life was much shorter and there was a child every year. The woman was worn out, she had nowhere to go and a shorter life expectancy. Now there are several stages of life as people live longer.

Politician: The question is: can you prevent the breakup of a coherent framework unit for kids when they are at a crucial stage?

Marketeer: In the past, men worked and brought home their pay to the wife (as is still the case in Japan). But she had no economic power on her own and had to stay in a relationship. Now women are getting more economic power. Women running the family finances is a long tradition. The fact that women can leave underlines their growing independence, but is it good for the family?

Technologist: Is it part of instant gratification and the "me" generation? The gap between expectations and delivery grows, so they leave.

> **Are family break-ups partly due to instant gratification and the "me" generation?**

Marketeer: In Nepal you trace your lineage through your mother because you can always be sure who your mother is. Men are visitors. Stability comes from the whole family unit but men are not expected to stay. The family as we know it with 2.3 kids, etc. is a Western tradition and a new one.

> **In Nepal you trace your lineage through your mother.**

Sociologist: History was more about arranged marriages, and that still is the case in some countries. And it meant that there were low expectations. Also, in the past the family acted as a work unit. But why did families stay stable in the face of the Industrial Revolution when the family work unit broke up?

Technologist: We are becoming a more secular society (Italy has a negative birth rate). Before, to be divorced had a strong social stigma.

Sociologist: Maybe society might authorize you as fit to reproduce, like a license. This would mean people would take marriage and reproduction more seriously, especially if there are stiff penalties for divorce where children are involved.

Marketeer: How about a children's charter? Everyone with a family must stick to it, children can report their parents if they violate it.

Politician: I suppose if we are going to see a change in the composition of the family then the design of houses will have to change if we aren't all mom, dad, and 2.4 kids. And what of all those single people who drift in and out of relationships? It means we are going to have a lot of supporting services such as dating agencies, counselling, psychotherapy, and yes, even spiritual tourism.

Economist: Those dating agencies are a scandal. There is likely to be more control exercised of these organizations in future.

Politician: If you abolish the family, you will have to accept more outside control – government or neo-government – someone who decides who looks after the children, etc. And there would have to be a collective provision for looking after the children: the kibbutz approach. As we have seen a move away from the nanny state, I can't see the government wanting to get more involved, unless non-secular institutions take over: the church, the mosque, or whatever.

Sociologist: I suspect that if men were to take a greater role in the bringing up of children, women may not feel so trapped. If teleworking takes off and men work more from home then this might change.

Marketeer: You could make a difference right away by valuing housework and child care better. Give it an economic added value.

The vectors of change – social

The ascent of women

The world is largely dominated and run by men. Women have traditionally been seen in the role of homemaking. The Western world has seen a gradually increasing role of women in the workforce and in management and key decision making. They are in some countries better educated than men and are achieving seniority earlier than men. If women are to continue their march towards taking an equal role to men in decision making then there are some important consequences for scenario plans. Female values are different to males and their needs as a customer grouping have to be treated differently. Here we look at some of those changing values.

A 1995 study published in the US *News and World Report* on the voting patterns of US women 75 years after they obtained voting rights provides some insights to the changing influence of women in society. It shows that the

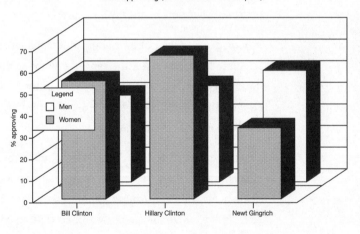

US voter preferences by gender

Those approving (*US News and World Report*)

gender gap between men and women continues to increase, with women voting more positively on caring issues such as welfare, health, education, and opportunity for all than men. It is estimated that nearly two-thirds of US women vote in opposition to their male partners.

As women find greater autonomy in their lives and they are able to express their own views either via the ballot box or via community-based organizations, then expect the value systems of most of the developed world to change.

Traditionally masculine values have been associated with wealth creation, protection of assets, supporting the male ego, and the triumph of confrontation over consensus. Female values have been associated with rearing family, caring for individuals and the community, and group consensus. These values are borne out by the finding that 30 percent of women approve of Gingrich's confrontational style versus over 50 percent of US men who approve.

In many parts of the developing world women's roles still have some way to go to achieve what US women have done in the last 100 years. The 1995 conference in Beijing highlighted some of the difficulties which women face: in Egypt, according to the Arab Women's Organization, it's legal to beat your wife provided she doesn't have to stay in hospital for more than 21 days. Women can be shot for not wearing the veil. Indian mothers abort the female foetus if they can predict the sex of their child before birth.

Brainstorming the consequences

Author: Women are voting more – what are the implications for political parties? If more women are in "women's" jobs, particularly in the public sector, does that make an impact on what policies they will vote for?

Technologist: But it is not translating into management. For the last 30 years it has been said that companies need the more feminine values of conciliation, teamwork, and empathy, but look at the top three levels of the major world companies and there are few women. In Europe less than 1% of board positions are occupied by women. So it sounds good, but it hasn't happened.

Sociologist: According to well-regarded opinion research, women are becoming more masculine, men more feminine. Women are taking more pleasure in violence. This female generation is also more committed to work. The gap of promotional opportunities is closing, while female professionals tend to be young and males older. Also, the number of women earning more than men has risen from 1 in 15 in the early 1980s to 1 in 5.

Marketeer: Women are now seen as central to decision-making about buying cars – women influence up to 70 percent of decisions on car buying. Women have had an influence too on nuclear issues, child care, community, and issue politics vs men in party politics.

Politician: Could this be the end of large hierarchical masculine organizations and the rise of smaller, more female friendly ones?

Marketeer: Services women need if they are working: cleaning, shopping, care of children, car maintenance. Men taking on female values: cosmetics, fashion.

Journalist: Female values are more caring, so we should expect more consumer checks on the ethical framework of companies/ethical credit cards, etc. Purchases where they make a contribution to society.

Actor: More women in stronger roles. Most of the highly paid actors are men at the moment because they get the strongest parts.

The vectors of change – technology

Commoditizing communications technology

Information technology has been the driver of change for many of us over the last 20 years. Will the next 20 years be as significant? Information technology has largely been a phenomenon of the developed world and the way the rest of the planet takes to it will be of interest not only to the providers of technology solutions but to most companies. Here we look at this important vector, which few people had heard of a generation ago.

Highlights

- *The world catches up*
- *The battle for content*
- *Content factories*
- *Implications for the consumer*
- *The death of the PC*

Popular themes

The world catches up. The Internet, opportunity or technoyawn? Will it kill the mall? Convergence in computing, communications, and media. Interconnectivity with all knowledge. Voice and thought recognition. Virtual reality. E-cash. Information crime. Nano technology. Technofashion. Informating products. Indian software factories.

■ The world catches up

It is said that in 1912 there were calls to close down the the US patents office as everything that was going to be invented had been invented: the car, the aeroplane, the light bulb, telephone, and so on. Today, over 80 years later, Japan alone registers some 500,000 patents a year, the US 150,000 and Europe some 80,000. Although we could hardly argue that the world is running short of inventions, there is considerable agreement amongst technology watchers that the world is going to take the next 10 to 20 years to catch up with what has already been invented.

Although the PC was introduced nearly 15 years ago and the much talked about Internet was developed on US Defense Department computers 30 years ago, fewer than 30 percent of American households have PCs, 15 percent have modems and 7 percent are connected to the Internet. Although PC sales are booming at some 15 million per annum, many of these in South-East Asia, the most optimistic guesses put the world PC-connected population at 50 million. That is 1 percent of those who have access to a telephone or TV. Although information technology is deeply embedded in the way most businesses operate, its use for the consumer is at a very early stage of development.

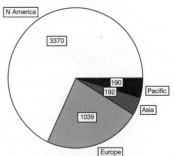

Internet hosts ('000s)
Source: The Internet Society

While one telephone was not much use to anyone, two telephones not marginally better, a community of telephone users began to create value in the technology. The value of any networked communication medium is proportional to the square of the number of users connected to the network. Like the fax, its value to the users and to the companies who provide goods and services through the medium increases the more people begin using the technology. The Internet is no exception to this rule. Up to 1994 most of the large commercial telephone carriers, network providers, and software companies dismissed the developing Internet-user community as a bunch of cranks. But with the user population effectively doubling every year and the number of host computers rising exponentially in the world to

> **But what is the likelihood that the Net goes the way of other communication technologies such as CB radio in the 1970s?**

around five million by 2000, everybody now is taking the Internet seriously. Telecommunication giants like AT&T, MCI, and BT are in the process of developing services to make the Net more reliable, secure, and responsive.

But what is the likelihood that the Net goes the way of other communication technologies such as CB radio in the 1970s? Here are a few hurdles to overcome:

● Its "signal to noise ratio," the ability to find what you're looking for, is poor.

- The quality and content of the information services on offer are unpoliceable at the moment. The US Senate is considering a bill to regulate porn and terrorist-related activities on the Net.
- It is running out of capacity and access to some of the bandwidth intensive services is discouragingly slow.
- Overcommercialization and control of the Net may actually dampen its growth, which has been fuelled by a chaotic, freeflowing, and sometimes subversive army of enthusiasts.

Despite these barriers there are enough reasons to believe *The Economist* when it says that "Open networking seems as fundamental to civilization's needs in the first half of the 21st century as ubiquitous, open roads did in the first half of the 20th." Many in the telecommunications industry believe that the volume of Internet traffic will have overtaken the existing voice communication by the turn of the century. Economist Brian Arthur at Stanford University has suggested that volume and the installed base for a technology provider gives it dominance in the market regarding technical standards and that this stifles competition and, more importantly, innovation. Unlike traditional consumer products which provide diminishing returns, a software provider actually increases dominance with growing market share. The Beta vs VHS battle for video and the IBM PC and the Apple standard bear this out.

When Microsoft wanted to merge with Intuit, the Californian law firm of Wilson, Sonsini, Goodrich, and Rosati used the increasing returns theory to convince the Justice Department that it should block the bid. If the deal had been approved, Microsoft could have been the world's biggest bank, running transactions directly from the PC on your desktop to your bank account.

Thousands of companies are at work today to make the Net easier to access. They have followed in the wake of the World Wide Web, which through its sound, graphics, and hypertext features has made navigating your way around the network not only fun but more productive. Others are working on increasing capacity and offering encryption facilities to make financial services less prone to fraud. Indeed, open networking could challenge the dominant position the telecommunication companies have had for the last half-century. With data, video, and even voice now available on the Net for a small proportion of what it costs on traditional commercial networks, the world's biggest telecommunication providers have one of the greatest challenges on their hands. The 1995 world telecommunications conference in Geneva gave the observer the feeling of chaos in an era of a dramatic increase in competition.

With the Internet's challenge to the long-distance market, user costs may be less related to distance and more a function of which network offers the easiest connectivity and features. Add to that companies like AT&T restructuring themselves to be more competitive and national phone companies in Europe announcing more competition in their supplier relationships, and there is a fear that the growth of new services such as multimedia will take a back seat while the industry reaches a point of some stability. Some observers argue that it might take more than 30 years before we see the real information age.

The 1995 world telecommunications conference in Geneva gave the observer the feeling of chaos

The question is, do traditional carriers continue as carriers or do they become content providers, offering news, entertainment, and other information-related services? A number have begun to position themselves for the latter. With the ability of the Internet to handle voice traffic, albeit crudely, industry experts are forecasting a day, in the not too distant future, when the giant telephone companies will be brought to their knees by the growth and increasing sophistication of the Net. Bill Gates has already given his verdict by saying, "I don't know why you would want to be in the long-distance market with that thing out there." VocalTec, a New Jersey company, is marketing software to enable users to make long-distance calls on the Net at a fraction of the cost of using the telephone.

It might take more than 30 years before we see the real information age.

If the Net does become the information highway of the future then it will have been a triumph for a non-commercial, community-based movement. It is probably the first advanced, technically driven mass-consumer product that has emerged in this way and may point the way for similar innovation in the future. It will also have proved yet again that the United States, which leads the world in its approach to deregulated market forces, continues to be the source of technical innovation in the world. A point of some envy to other nations and one which will ensure that North America continues to be economically strong.

I don't know why you would want to be in the long-distance market.

INTERNET PROFILES

- 85 percent male
- Average earnings $30,000
- Spends 10 hours a week in Cyberspace
- He is a browser not yet a buyer
- Sex is the most popular content accessed
- Of 25 most popular sites, 10 are based around sex

Advertising on the Net

Although the Internet has some way to go to become a well understood and accepted medium for advertising, unlike traditional media, the Internet offers a two-way means of communication. In other words if I see an ad on USA Today's digital pages, pointing and clicking will route me through to a detailed set of information on the product. I could if I wanted either order more product literature or the product itself. Advertising in USA Today's mass circulation newspaper doesn't give the advertiser any indication of how many people actually saw the ad. Independent organizations are cropping up which offers to audit the number of "hits" achieved for an ad, and some sites are offering payment conditions based on the number of hits or interactions with prospective customers. This type of one-to-one advertising promises to revolutionize the advertising industry.

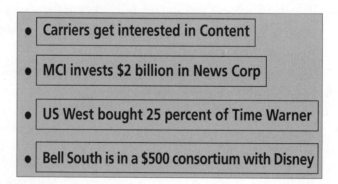

- Carriers get interested in Content
- MCI invests $2 billion in News Corp
- US West bought 25 percent of Time Warner
- Bell South is in a $500 consortium with Disney

■ The battle for content

With the proliferation of distribution outlets for media, content and, in particular, quality content will be in short supply. With cable companies offering hundreds of channels to choose from, and the future availability of video over the Internet, the commoditization of distribution is a strong possibility. Content will increasingly be the future battleground for viewing market share. Content providers are already enjoying a boom in prices for their programs.

> "Steven Spielberg would be as good at running a telecoms company as Ray Smith (CEO Bell Atlantic)"
>
> *Nicholas Negroponte*

The providers will draw from a wider range of subjects to entertain people than ever before. From Shakespeare to sleaze, program makers will continuously push the boundaries of what is socially acceptable and popular. TFI, the French satellite channel, recently ran Saturday night live chat shows which crossed the boundary of decency by miles. Although the show was criticized for being sexually over-explicit and racially offensive to the country's Algerian community, it drew over 20 percent of the viewing population.

Content factories

When Jeffrey Katzenberg, Steven Spielberg, and David Geffen combined their creative talents to form a new studio, Dreamworks, the trio signaled the rebirth of animation production or content factories to meet the insatiable demand for full-length animated features. The studio poached top animators from rival studios, creating a salary war for some of the top creatives in toon town.

When 39-year-old Pete Weston went to school he told his parents he wanted to draw cartoons for a living. "They told me I'd starve," says Weston, a Londoner who has animated for some of the greatest Disney classics in the last decade. "Today, I'm busier and more in demand than I've ever been. The guys who went off to be engineers, chemists, and accountants are struggling to keep out of negative equity." With animators enjoying top star status on a par with some of the biggest screen names and salaries in the $200,000 league, the cost of content will undoubtedly escalate. Competition amongst the top studios of Disney, Time Warner, Warner Bros, Twentieth Century Fox, Turner Pictures, and Dreamworks will bring a new lease of life to the cartoon in the next century.

> *Today, animators are more in demand than they've ever been.*

■ Implications for the consumer

These are some of the implications for the consumer by the end of this century:

Convergence will have ensured that the PC becomes the window through which we shop, bank, learn, and entertain ourselves. Expect PC design and packaging to begin to meet the consumers' requirements for these services. In addition to the "PC in every room" phenomenon we will see PCs in every shape and form emerging in the home. There could be around 200 million PCs by 2005. The miniaturization of the PC and its specialization for specific functions such as banking or shopping will begin to be offered.

As companies are finding, offering services on the Net allows the smallest organizations to compete with large ones. A company can start a record label offering recordings of its artists without the substantial distribution and packaging costs of the traditional physical format. Similarly, insurance providers can quote for cover directly to the user without the need for intermediaries.

> *In addition to the "PC in every room" phenomenon we will see PCs in every shape and form emerging in the home.*

Whilst the small newcomers can challenge the traditional players by their speed, flexibility, and better understanding of the Net user, big corporations can handle scale with greater ease. Thus an organization offering banking services can open up a global market of a hundred million customers or more at a fraction of the cost of a physical network as all transactions are paperless. It is likely that the historical demarcations of a bank, a networking company, or a software house will disappear and that each organization will challenge each other for dominance of share-of-the-customer's business. Microsoft may well offer banking or entertainment from its origins as a software house

The customer is likely to go through a stage of confusion as age-old preconceptions about where to shop or obtain services are changed. Younger users are more likely to adapt to these structural changes than their older counterparts. Today's mail order demand, in the order of 5 percent in Germany, for example, is small and frequently at the lower end of the market. It remains to be seen if new remote shopping technology will improve service to a significant level so as to result in a step change in demand.

The increased interactivity brought about by the Net will spawn new thinking about the way we deliver news and information. Bob Crozier, President of *Fortune* in Europe, says that within a couple of hours of the magazine going live on the Net a quarter of a million "hits" have been registered. And within a further couple of hours readers have begun to correspond with the authors of feature articles, commenting, criticizing, or challenging points of detail. The authors then have the opportunity to respond to their readers in real time. Are we seeing the genesis of the real-time newspaper?

The interactivity of the Net will allow the growth of consumer groups, sociopolitical activists, and "virtual communities" to influence politicians and corporations. Witness the success of Greenpeace in their campaign against Shell

> *Are we seeing the genesis of the real-time newspaper?*

in the Brent Spar incident. Within days, Greenpeace had put its case to its sympathizers across Europe and the boycott of Shell service stations had begun.

Companies will run electronic shop fronts on behalf of retailers. These may run as franchise operations with the franchisee being trained by the retailer in all aspects of the product. Services such as Marketplace-MCI, an electronic mall, create the illusion of a shopping mall as the "shop-

> *Companies will run electronic shop fronts on behalf of retailers.*

per" browses from store to store. Imagine Macy's, Harrods, Safeway, and even nuts-and-bolts Woolworth displaying their wares anywhere on the network.

Others will offer directories and help-line facilities. The Net will continue to baffle the non-techie for some time to come and the mushrooming popularity of being wired, of having an electronic address on your business card, and of pressure from friends and relatives will force the uninitiated to join the club. These users will be perfect targets for such services.

Although the Net may be one of the fundamental developments in communications to change our lives, its speed of take-up is impossible to predict. A *Wall Street Journal* article by Daniel Pearl describes how at the turn of the last century futurologists said that the telephone would bring peace on earth, revolutionize surgery, and save agriculture by making farmers less lonely. According to SC Gilfillan, a technology watcher of the time, a "home theater" would allow people to dial up symphonies, speeches, and 3-D Shakespeare plays. Novels, movie theatres, and governments might vanish in the process. Hopefully we won't have to wait another hundred years to realize some of those predictions.

The anarchy of the Internet: virtual communities

One powerful force eroding the once-rigid boundaries of countries is the virtual communities springing up on the Internet. People around the world, with

> *Services on the Net could become like a 19th-century Eastern bazaar, a mixture of bargains, fakes and rip-offs, but great fun to browse through.*

common interests stretching from train spotting to bee keeping, keep in touch through their modems. Services on the Net could become like a 19th-century Eastern bazaar. Unregulated, no guarantees on quality or delivery, a mixture of bargains, fakes and rip-offs, but great fun to browse through because of the diversity and range of products.

Information crime

The movement of cash electronically has begun to give rise to a new breed of thief: the electronic hacker. The case of global fraud disclosed by Citicorp, where $12 million were moved from corporate funds illegally by a Russian hacker in St Petersburg, depicts a problem which will be increasingly difficult to control. The bank, which moves $500 billion a day around the world, was alerted to the incident by a corporate customer in Argentina who watched on a screen funds being illegally transferred out to an unauthorized account in California. Apparently Citicorp's multilevel security system and its rigorous controls were no barrier to a competent hacker. Information crime is transparent, it is not accompanied by violence, it can be perpetrated by criminals thousands of miles away, and it appears that at the moment there are few rapid response international policing procedures in place to catch criminals. It is impossible to estimate the extent of cash which is moved illegally, partly because the banks may not know, and partly because if they did know they would not publicize the fact.

Bangalore

Of India's approximately $2 billion in information technology revenues, about a quarter comes from software and most of it seems to be congregated in the city of Bangalore where salaries have rocketed and the local infrastructure has begun to lag behind the rapid expansion since 1991. But so far Bangalore has only managed to penetrate the contract software markets of the West, with bodyshop operations making a killing at home and abroad by shipping thousands of Indian programmers to the US at rates that are about a fifth of those in North America; a veritable "software slave trade." Without products to sell to the West, Bangalore could be the future software factory for the world but lacking the value-added products which have given Microsoft, Oracle and SAP world dominance.

Informating products

Automobile manufacturers have used computer chips to monitor and record vehicle performance so that during use and at the time of servicing the car, information on performance can be used to optimize its efficiency. This has been followed up by tyre manufacturers experimenting with microchips impregnated in the tread to monitor how the tyre stands up to wear and tear. The recorded information can then be used to improve product design. Cheap throw-away chip technology could bring this feature of informating products to many of the everyday goods we use including sports shoes and equipment, affinity cards and household consumer durables.

The death of the PC

The end of the PC may be closer than we think. As one expert recently commented, "It's as daft as expecting a device in your kitchen to peel the potatoes, do the cooking, the washing-up and dry up afterwards. The PC is being expected to be a banker, an entertainer, a postman, and an office organizer all rolled into one. Its functions may have become overloaded, making it an unacceptably complex device."

> **The end of the PC may be closer than we think.**

It is the availability of software down the Net that could be the death of the PC as we know it today. The big debate between Bill Gates of Microsoft and Larry Ellison, head of Oracle, put this into context. Gates has predicted the rise and rise of the PC supported by his Windows software while Ellison has plumbed for the cheap terminal option. The latter has suggested that Apple's best move in the future would be into producing inexpensive terminals, or in other words network appliances, at around $200 a throw.

A major driver is that PC-users are becoming disillusioned by the rapid obsolescence in the software and equipment they buy. The launch of Windows 95 gave rise to much criticism by many first-time users that one needed the services of trained operators to load and run the sofware. One computer expert reminded his clients that Microsoft's new software operating system was larger and more complicated than mainframe equivalents ten years ago.

Cheap computer terminals could download programs from a network with the benefit to the user of the most up-to-date version being available. The supplier of the software and the network provider would benefit from frequency of usage with a spin-off advantage of being able to get ahead of the software pirates who sell illegal copies today in the flea-markets of Asia at one-twentieth of the cost of the legal item.

Brainstorming the consequences

Will the Internet turn out to be permanent, or end up like CB radio?

Technologist: It is here to stay. It might be imperfect, chaotic, but they will pile in because you can see how it can be upgraded bit by bit. Like security – that is already being solved. Bandwidths? That will be dealt with. But who will initiate this? The people affected, the owners of the various services. Yes, it is a chaotic phenomenon but a lot of technical issues have been solved in a very effective way outside the normal standards arena. So a new way of working has started to emerge. Some are technical people in universities, some are suppliers, some are in telephone companies.

Author: This is communitarianism in practice. But when you get to the next step up, does it get bogged down when the big boys pile in and big company issues come in?

> **Its chaos is its strength.**

Sociologist: It is reckoned that most services will be paid for by advertising, with pages on the World Wide Web. It creates a true one-to-one relationship and gets beyond direct mail. It is like both the Agricultural and Industrial revolutions, where initial chaos was transformed when big interests came in? Once companies like American Express come in, it gets transformed.

> **I think PCs will be like Swatch watches.**

Economist: Its chaos is its strength. The Industrial Revolution has never plateaued, after all.

Politician: If you applied the progress in computers to transportation, you would be able to fly at several light years speed.

Technologist: I think PCs will be like Swatch watches vs more expensive ones – you will have a whole variety of different products. Also, increasingly in the middle to upper ranges, the consumers will become more precise in their needs. There will be more specific products depending on use.

> **When Concorde is withdrawn from service it will mean for the first time since the wheel was invented mankind has gone slower in public transport.**

Politician: Do you realize that if airlines take Concorde out of operation, in 2005 or whenever, that will mean for the first time since the wheel was invented mankind has gone slower in public transport rather than faster. There is no supersonic transportation system set to take over. But is technology taking over transport?

The vectors of change – technology

The fragile earth

The environment is another vector which probably would not have featured in a book like this 30 years ago. Today the impact of the way we treat our fragile world is beginning to be understood and the futurist is acutely aware that the past freedoms that have been available to us will no longer exist. For how much longer will we be able to dump millions of tons of carbon into the atmosphere? How much longer before we can't find anywhere to dump our waste? What will be the fall-out of the next big environmental disaster? We provide clues to these and other questions below.

Highlights

- *Rising concern*
- *Waste management*
- *Garbage theft*
- *Lower atmosphere pollution*
- *Nuclear power – a disaster waiting to happen*
- *Pressure points on the environment*
- *Waste management, recycling, packaging, emissions, nuclear reactors*

■ Rising concern

The pressures on the environment from a rapidly industrializing world have been much publicized. There are different opinions as to the exact effect the CO_2, CFCs, SO_2, and numerous other toxic emissions have on the environment. What we are sure of is that we have been witness-

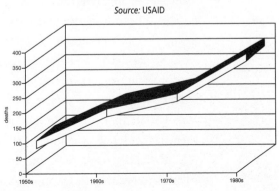

Weather disasters (>20 deaths)
Source: USAID

ing a change in weather patterns over the last 20 years to more extremes. We have witnessed some of the warmest years on record in the last 20 years. The seas have risen to record levels in many areas of the world causing destruction of coastal areas. The waves in the North Sea are today 50 percent higher than recorded 20 years ago. The number and intensity of earthquakes in certain areas such as California have increased by five or six times over the last decade

> **Human activity is definitely contributing to the greenhouse effect.**

These megadisasters have begun to take concern for the environment out of the circle of fringe green politics to a wider population. Opinion polls around the world show widespread concern about the future of the environment. Increasingly people are prepared to take action as customers against companies believed to be harming the environment. Lately the UN Intergovernmental Panel on Climate Change (IPCC), one of the most respected bodies looking at the effects of global warming, has concluded that human activity is definitely contributing to the greenhouse effect. It calls for drastic cuts in man-made gas emissions. Any response to this call for significant reductions in emissions has to be considered together with an equivalent reduction in economic activity worldwide. This is an argument which both developing and advanced economies of the world will find difficult to agree on.

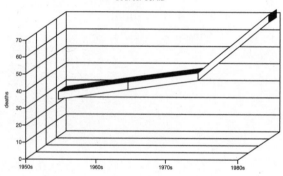

Typhoons (>20 deaths)

Source: USAID

The Brent Spar incident in 1995 is a good case study in the power of the consumer against a multinational, in this case Shell. Without seeking to take sides in this episode, the events leading to Shell reversing its decision to sink a platform in one and a half miles of deep water in the North Sea were brought about by a major boycott of Shell service stations in continental Europe. The organization of this mass boycott was the work of Greenpeace activists who were so effective in their campaign that Mori polls taken suggested that an overwhelming majority of people trusted the Greenpeace scientific evidence in favour of the Shell or UK Government experts.

McDonald's took two unemployed activists to court in the UK in an attempt to get them to stop a campaign of leaflets they distributed at outlets alleging that the company was responsible for the destruction of rain forests. Cattle, grazing on these lands, they alleged, were the source of beef in their hamburgers. Two years and several millions of dollars later the action has not been resolved and McDonald's appears to have dug its heels in for a protracted battle. In the meantime, the publicity caused by the action and the ineffectual sanctions that the company can bring to bear on the two protagonists put in doubt this company's strategy in dealing with environmental activism.

> *Even companies who have differentiated themselves for their green credentials are not immune to criticism.*

Even companies who have differentiated themselves for their green credentials are not immune to criticism. Anita Roddick's Body Shop took a good deal of negative publicity for alleged infringements of their policy of not testing cosmetics on animals and the exploitation of Third World suppliers. Its stock price fell and it took nearly a year for the management of the company to recover from the allegations.

There is a wide gap between business and organizations like Greenpeace on how to treat the environment. Business sees the latter more concerned with making sensationalist headlines as a means of progressing the environmental cause, whilst the latter sees business as putting short-term profit before the preservation of the planet.

> *Procter & Gamble uses its "more from less" program to promote better waste management.*

A few corporations have begun to introduce economic arguments to justify environmental considerations into their organizations. Procter & Gamble uses its "more from less" program to promote better waste management, power-generating companies and petrochemical producers see environmental control as a prerequisite to risk management and their license to operate, and many consumer product suppliers see the need to publish environmental charters as a means of maintaining customer retention.

> *Virtual communities like Greenpeace have begun to act as a powerful force of change.*

Companies will need to involve environmental lobby groups much more in future to develop environmental strategies no matter how ethically correct the companies' own planners believe they are. It will call for greater transparency of information on a company's approach to environmental issues and this may spawn services such as an environmental audit involving an annual scrutiny of a company's operations. We may see activist groups such as Greenpeace participating in such exercises.

■ Waste management

The amount of disposable waste produced per head of the US population is 1,500 pounds, whilst every European produces some 700 pounds each year. This waste is processed in a variety of ways: some of it is incinerated, some of it dumped in the sea or on land-fill sites. The number of available sites is decreasing around the world, and communities living near these sites are forming strongly vocal groups to oppose the siting of new sites near them. By encouraging recycling, the City of Los Angeles has since 1990 made significant efforts to reduce the amount of waste from garbage cans by 30 percent.

Perhaps the greatest concern in waste disposal is voiced by companies in the waste management business. An executive from Waste Management Inc, a US-parented company expanding its operations in Europe, speaks of the lax legislation that exists in Europe on the disposal of waste. The problem is likely to manifest itself in a major ecological disaster such as toxins leaking into an underground aquifers and causing death and possibly a national emergency in the country where it occurs. Such a disaster would eventually tighten up legislation and control.

Already packaging of consumer products is under scrutiny by both governments and consumer groups and retailers may begin to differentiate themselves on the environmental friendliness of their packaging. Biodegradable cartons, bags, and containers, for example, may be areas where consumers are attracted to one retailer over another.

■ Garbage theft

City police in Los Angeles have been brought in to stop the theft of garbage worth $2 million from the city's waste bins. With the price of old newsprint rising to a peak of $200 a ton, unofficial scavengers have been doing their dark deeds at night whilst the city sleeps and before the official collectors come for their trash in the morning. Recyclable waste is becoming valuable, partly encouraged by legislation and partly by scarcity of raw materials. Newsprint prices have been rising 40 percent year on year.

■ Lower atmosphere pollution

Some of the world's biggest cities are becoming death traps for the young and elderly. Thousands are affected by respiratory illnesses, and during a prolonged hot spell of weather with little wind even cities like London are begining to join the ranks of the long-term trouble spots of Mexico City and Los Angeles. We should increasingly see cities substantially curbing the internal combustion engine in favour of low-emission transportation systems. California has tried to institute a law which requires that all auto manufacturers in the state ensure that 2 percent of their cars emit no pollutants. Electric cars are regarded as having no pollutants.

In a poll of Berliners 47 percent of them said that given the choice they would live in a car-free environment. A further 15 percent said that they would also elect to do so if they could get to their car within a distance of half a kilometer. After a second year of record pollution levels in Europe's 70 largest cities, where in nearly 3,000 cases ozone levels exceeded the European Union's recommendations, community groups and politicians are calling for significant restrictions to the car. Influential members of Germany's coalition parties have called for all motor vehicles to be fitted with catalytic converters by the year 2000.

Although the electricity for cars which is produced in fossil-fuel power stations is only 30 percent efficient, batteries deliver more effective propulsion in slow-moving traffic. GM estimates that an electric car is overall 60 percent more efficient than its petroleum equivalent.

Here are some of the ways in which exhaust emission controls could affect our lives:

- Loss of freedom to use the car whenever and wherever we like.
- An increase in the number of areas where we will not be able to take a car.
- Pressure to use mass transport systems.
- Incentives to use smaller, low-emission cars.

■ Nuclear power – a disaster waiting to happen?

In the spring of 1986 the world witnessed the biggest civilian nuclear disaster at the Chernobyl power station in the Ukraine. Today, according to experts, the remaining two of the four reactors are amongst the five most unsafe plants in the world. Yet the state can ill afford to shut it down completely. The facility provides 7 percent of the energy for the Ukraine and with disputes over oil and gas supplies with Russia and the $4 billion cost of clean-up and alternative provision, help needs to come from the richest countries in the G7 to provide a solution.

Brainstorming the consequences

Does the shrinking world mean that all organizations have to take environmental behavior into account wherever they are located?

Technologist: I think all companies have to be aware of the inherent PR risk in their operations. Public opinion can move very fast. Look at Shell and Brent Spar, Shell and Nigeria. People were being encouraged not to buy French products because of nuclear testing. It spreads quickly.

Marketeer: In terms of environmental impact, companies like Dow Corning have to take it into account the cradle to grave consequences of their products.

Actor: More people that I know in London are not using their cars. It almost becomes socially unacceptable to use your car for short journeys, just as it is to smoke in meetings. But the problem is that we have created such a strong car culture that it is very hard to give it up.

Sociologist: I think technology will ultimately solve the problems, as companies realize there is a lot of money to be made in finding solutions to environmental problems more are coming in.

Economist: German companies are way ahead in thinking about the environmental impact. This is the model that is beginning to spread around Europe.

Author: But will all this come too late? If you look at the pollution in Eastern Europe and the CIS, it is pretty damaging. Some lakes in Russia are literally dead.

Technologist: And you don't see the Chinese or North Koreans organizing protests against pollution. Partly because the state would suppress any protest and partly because when people are struggling to industrialise rapidly, environmentalism slows them down.

Technologist from Britain: If you look at the sort of people who were protesting about exporting live veal calves to France, they were all ages and all classes. Children today are far more aware of the issues than we were at that age.

Economist: Environmental problems do not know borders, so they really have to be addressed by a world body. But which one has enough clout and willpower?

Marketeer: One problem is that people care about the environment globally, and accuse big companies of misdemeanors, but they don't always translate their worries into their daily behavior. Does everyone recycle or buy products which are environmentally friendly?

The vectors of change – technology

Competition for education

Last but not least we end with education, the vector which raises expectations and prepares citizens for life. Employers and educators will need to look at the future of education to anticipate the needs of society and the new professions which probably haven't been invented yet. Educators have been continually criticized for not keeping step with market demand, and scenario planning may be perhaps most appropriate for their purposes.

Highlights

- *Life-long learning*
- *Education and the information age*
- *Globalizing education*
- *The rise in the perceived value of education. Knowledge-rich products. Literacy rates decreasing. Remote learning.*

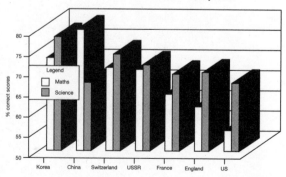

World proficiency scores
Source: Cremers, Swint, Reynolds

■ Life-long learning

The concept of life-long learning comes from the belief that the pace of change in the future will require individuals to continually update their skills. This may either be brought about by a fall in demand for a particular skill and the need to retrain or acquire new knowledge, or the need to update existing professional skills. Many of the marketing graduates of today may not be equipped for the one-to-one marketing techniques of the future; equally unemployed economists may need to retrain in other areas such as journalism or communications to ensure continued employment.

The responsibility for learning in organizations is shifting rapidly to the individual. More than 50 percent of all education in most European organizations is identified by individual members of staff developing their own training needs program. Educational institutions will have to evolve market research techniques and continual review mechanisms of their curricula to keep pace with this change.

Educators in the West are caught up in the debate on the dwindling resources being made available to educate children. Class ratios of teacher to pupils, it is argued, are closely related to educational achievement; the fewer the pupils, the better their learning. Yet in examining the world benchmarks of national achievement on comparable subjects such as maths and science, countries with far fewer educational resources score significantly higher marks. It is becoming clear to some educators that attitude to education and the value of it to a society is one of the key drivers to successful educational achievement. Politicians in the West are talking of introducing fines to parents whose children play truant regularly.

■ Education and the information age

There is a growing interest amongst politicians in promoting the use of information technology in education. Heidi and Alvin Toffler have become household names for their series of books which have promoted the new information age. Newt Gingrich, the Speaker of the US House of Representatives, promotes the need for the US to be at the leading edge of the information revolution by stepping up the investment in educational programs which enhance citizens' IT knowledge. Tony Blair, Britain's Labour Party leader, has proposed a partnership with British Telecom to provide a national information highway connecting all schools and libraries in exchange for liberalizing the laws which prevent the company from entering the entertainment market.

■ Globalizing education

So far, if you wanted a degree from Harvard or MIT, you had to apply to get on a course there, get accepted, and then do a stint of, say, two years before you could use the coveted letters MBA after your name. The cost is upwards of $60,000 all in. With many more people today chasing top schools around the world, there are waiting lists of several years for some programs and many disappointed students.

With many educational institutions around the world offering distance learning courses, the only technical barrier to interactive distance learning is the network which might eventually connect students to the top schools in the world. The only other obstacle is the ability of the institutions themselves to react to the opportunities created by the new communications technology.

Already, Europe's first cyberspace campus has been opened in north-eastern Spain. They plan to have over 10,000 students at the turn of the century taking courses in a wide range of subjects. Students will be able to access course modules, conduct research, clarify ideas and problems, submit course work, and be examined on the network. If students can carry out all these activities in and around Barcelona, the Harvard MBA acquired in cyberspace is close behind. Students will be able to acquire world class learning thousands of miles away and probably at a fraction of the cost of the "real" thing. In fact the globalization of education will give rise to more privately funded universities and schools. "When the percentage of overseas students is overwhelmingly greater than country nationals at your top educational institutions, you have to wonder if government funding is appropriate," said the dean of one European university.

> **The Harvard MBA acquired in cyberspace is close behind.**

Brainstorming the consequences

Technologist: A big issue is getting people IT literate and wired so they can become part of society. There are big initiatives with a number of governments across Europe to improve the access to IT in the schools and also to improve it in places like libraries and local government, so people will get used to it. So it is a question of access and the information you can get from it. This will be part of an attitude change.

But IT isn't enough. There was a very interesting experiment done in Moscow. They had no PCs at all until three years ago. They arrived, and a professor studied 50 families. Half used books to find things out, half didn't. All were given a PC. The half who used books used the PCs to find things out and the half that didn't use books used the PCs to play games. So access will not necessarily change attitudes. But without access you will be cut off from so much information. So it is necessary but not sufficient.

So the decline will be accelerated without access. One is the physical lack of access, and the other is mental – the assumption that there is information there to get, but you can't get at it.

Politician: Isn't all this the key to getting rid of the two-tier? The bottom tier can find school very boring. Education is not interesting or meaningful. So using new technology they find it can get through to them. It also means that programs can be designed to go at their own speed. And the quality is increasing all the time. It also can overcome bad teaching. Education as fun.

> *This is not about replacing teachers but relating to children.*

Technologist: This is not about replacing teachers but relating to children and using IT to teach them subjects which are difficult, like maths.

Politician: When the Open University started, the idea was they could get the best professors in the world on to TV and everyone could get access to a university education. But it isn't like that, even with the best written material. They have had to get human contact or it doesn't gel.

TWO SCENARIOS FOR 2015

In this part we develop two scenarios for 2015 based on the emerging themes in the vectors of change and the brainstorming sessions. We deal with each one in turn and show news coverage depicting each scenario. We have used a scene in a café to illustrate the mid-life scenario. There are in all 17 vectors depicted in the illustration. See if you can spot them.

The Mid-Life Café

Adrian Chesterman

The vectors of change depicted in the café: *The privatization of welfare, the global teenager, preserving the family, the ascent of women, life-long learning, communitarianism, portfolio workers, E-cash, the solitaire, healthy living, globalization of brands, Asian consumerism, down-ageing products, environmentalism and electric transport, alternative religions, pensioners get back to work and the back-lash to the gerontocracy.*

The world in mid-life crisis scenario

Summary

The developed world with its relatively ageing population will have difficulty coping with its lost youth and envy the younger populations of the emerging world. Places will begin to take on the look of Miami, Bournemouth, or Vichy. Conservatism will dominate fashion, politics, product design, and the media, with down-ageing products to extend the feeling of youth. Western cultures will become more thoughtful and sensitive about their environment, nurture stronger female qualities of introspection and increase savings rates to plan for old age. There could be a religious revival and a renaissance of the arts. We will see an increase of women in leadership positions. Meanwhile the emerging world with its younger populations will begin to challenge its older citizens who control power and influence. These older citizens will exert considerable force to keep, where possible, traditional values challenged by global television and mass Western-styled advertising.

■ Mid-life crisis

Today half the world is under 20 years of age but most of those young people live in the poorer countries of the world. The developed world, where most of the economic power resides, has an ageing population and it will be getting even older over the next 20 years. We have referred to this scenario as the World in Mid-life Crisis because the situation resembles a mature adult reaching mid-life. According to Jung the individual approaching mid-life exhibits the following characteristics:

- The individual reaches a stage when conservatism creeps into one's thinking and dramatic change is generally avoided. This is not the time to think about revolutionary ideals or changing society or world order.
- There is some regret at the life that perhaps the individual did not manage to lead or the places that he or she did not visit. There may be a craving for

buying that sports car that was always previously out of reach or seeking sexual fulfillment with younger partners where this may be lacking in existing relationships.

- The male takes on feminine qualities of sensitivity, caring, and sharing, whilst the female takes on action-oriented male qualities of leadership, business building, and wealth creation. This may manifest itself by men giving up their careers to start anew. Women, on the other hand, having spent most of their adulthood caring for the family, will begin new lucrative careers.

It is with this background in mind that we have constructed the mid-life scenario. We will explore how the world might react to the vectors of change which we currently face in the world, and although some of the eventual conclusions to a particular driving force may sound incredible, this has been done to make a point of the extreme outcomes.

■ The family

> **Laws making it difficult to get a divorce will be enacted.**

The breakdown of the family as seen by society will give increasing cause for concern. Citizens will not want the marriage tradition, which goes back thousands of years, to be destroyed in a couple of decades. The rise in single-parent families, the numerous broken homes, and the resultant effect on children underperforming at school and taking to drug-related crime will be blamed on the breakup of family systems. Politicians, communities, and even corporations will join in unison to reverse the trend. Laws making it difficult to get a divorce will be enacted, with judges having the power to enforce cooling-off periods and reconciliation. Huge financial disincentives will be introduced, particularly where children are involved, to make couples think twice before making the break. In order to avoid the negative impact of cohabiting couples avoiding marriage because of the restrictions on separation, governments will introduce generous tax incentives for couples to be married and in addition financial encouragement will be given to married couples in the developed world to have children. Japan, Germany, and Italy will face a demographic time bomb unless they encourage their citizens to step up procreation.

> **The commercial sector will respond accordingly with "marriage is good" messages.**

The commercial sector will respond accordingly with "marriage is good" messages. Films like the remakes of *Sleepless in Seattle*, and *Forget Paris* will revive the 1930's romantic Hollywood themes which filled the silver screen at the time. Consumer-product companies will also exploit the family theme from "Happy family" cornflakes to "Family value" hamburgers. Vacation and tour promoters will also promote special "family friendly" holidays in parts of the world where it has previously only been possible to travel if you are single and unattached.

Insurance providers will provide family protection policies which give generous pay-outs, tax free on a couple reaching their silver wedding anniversary. Like in the US, the president or prime minister of a country may send a special telegram to those celebrating 50 years in married bliss.

The extended family becomes fashionable again.

The extended family becomes fashionable again. No longer only is it considered cool to have mum and dad live next door, but there are good tax breaks too. Homes are extended or specially designed to house a "granny annex" and the resale value of homes with these facilities is substantially enhanced.

In Asia, elderly statesmen become concerned about the degradation in family values brought about by television and the projection of Western moral values. Singapore steps up its family protection program, stressing the need for women to show responsibility towards their community and nation. Men are told to respect the role that women have to play in the home. Severe financial constraints are placed on couples who decide to separate, including the need for both parties to publish an advertisement in the press telling the community the reasons for their separation and asking them their forgiveness for having broken a marriage contract. Funding for government dating agencies is stepped up in an effort to increase the marriage rate.

Funding for government dating agencies is stepped up in an effort to increase the marriage rate.

Young Indian women have begun to rebel against the arranged marriage, influenced by the media and by the strengthening of their roles in business and commerce. Marrying for love rather than compatibility goes against the grain of Indian tradition and is grudgingly accepted in more affluent families as the way of the modern world. Religious leaders lobby hard for a say in giving their blessing to all marriages in an effort to ensure traditional parental influence in the bride's choice is maintained.

Young Indian women have begun to rebel against the arranged marriage.

Outcomes

The European Union incorporates a new amendment into its charter which puts an economic value on housework. Looking after the children, taking them to school, and categories of homemaking are given a value. The value is assessed in relation to what it would cost to provide these services via childminders and domestic workers. These would be added to GDP calculations when assessing real growth in the economy.

An economic value on housework.

THE MID-LIFE ⧗ TIMES

January 1, 2015

Marriage stages major comeback – divorce rate falls for first time this century

The office of census and surveys revealed one of the best set of statistics for countries in the North Atlantic as a special new year present. For the first time since the middle of the last century the number of recorded marriages rose by 5 percent over the last year.

A spokesperson for the authority was quoted as saying, "These figures would seem to vindicate the aggressive family values programs pursued by governments since the beginning of this century, when the number of marriages had fallen to an all-time low."

Evidence that the compulsory counseling program for couples considering divorce has succeeded was also borne out by the fourth year's consecutive fall in the number of divorces granted by the courts.

Under current law couples with children aged under 16 have to apply to a government tribunal for divorce. Only in exceptional circumstances will a tribunal allow a divorce unless it is satisfied that the couple have undergone a cooling-off period of at least one year and have agreed to attend three residential counseling sessions with a government-approved counselor.

Although the news was welcomed by community and church leaders, Action Against Males, a feminist organization, dismissed the report as being a fabrication to hide the deep injustice being perpetrated against women. "We have lost the woman's right to choose her own future. Many women are having to suffer the indignity of both physical and mental torture in their homes for the benefit of men."

Romance is in the air once more

Lonely, unattached?
Call 0800-FAM 1 LY

GRANNY FLATS HOLD PREMIUM

Despite the recent slump in house prices those with customized facilities for the elderly or live-in parents have held their prices up well according to a survey by the Moynihan Institute, a research-based foundation promoting family values.

Most families seeking to support their parents make do with a spare room in the house with the two children having to forfeit a bedroom of their own.

"Homes that offer self-contained accommodation for parents are at a higher premium as there is more space for the three different generations to get on with life without falling over each other."

Love is a Many Splendoured Thing scoops Oscars

The remake of the 1950s Hollywood romantic tear-jerker made a comeback 65 years later as the best film of 2014.

Worldwide audiences on Twenty-First Century Entertainments interactive channel were independently audited at 247 million, the highest since records began.

Club 4+2 launches exotic destination program

One of Club 4+2's exotic destinations

Club 4+2, the highly successful vacation company which has targeted the extended family segment with its Mediterranean resort program, has now extended its new season offers to long-haul destinations in Asia.

The company, founded in 2005 by entrepreneur and former Catholic priest, Michael Shannon, has been successful at targeting the fast-growing sector of families which have invited mum and dad to live with them. The company discounts heavily the price of the two additional adults provided at least two full-price holidays are purchased.

Michael, himself a married man with parents who live in, was the centre of criticism by the church in Ireland last year after he published a series of advertisements in the Irish press calling for the "primitive" abolition of the restrictions imposed on priests not to marry. Shannon claimed that the position taken by the church was anti-family and against the teachings of Christ.

■ Jobs

Because the over-60s have become aware that they have to work to continue to fund their inadequate pensions, they re-enter the workforce late in life. They are welcomed by employers who discover that they have management and organizational skills which their younger counterparts lack.

The large office in central city locations has become a rare occurrence. The realization that the office is one of the least utilized assets leads employers to reconsider alternative means of locating employees. Approximately 30 percent work from home, many of these women, who find the arrangement convenient to bring up a family in the early years of their childhood. A further 10–20 percent work from neighborhood work centres and at least one major bank has embarked on a "total life-cycle needs" strategy, which involves offering customers office facilities in their neighborhood shopping centers. With the advent of automated, remote banking, the bank no longer needs the physical buildings which once housed cashiers and office administrators. Selling off the assets didn't seem to make sense because of the dramatic fall in property due to the drift away from town centers to out of town shopping and remote shopping. People working as self-employed individuals or in small groups of networked associates make good use of these facilities.

Approximately 30 percent work from home.

Not only can you make use of high-speed communication links with the rest of the world at these neighborhood centers, but you can also make use of a range of support services from marketing advice, design and production of digital brochures, accounting and finance services to help track your receipts, payments, and tax returns. Here you may rub shoulders with an economist, a marketeer, a software engineer, or a financial adviser at the coffee dispenser. Two things bind you together: the network of contacts to find out where there is work, and the neighborhood you live in – your children, for example, go to the same school.

The jobs drift away to lower-cost areas has slowed to a trickle.

The bank also provides a marketing service to those registered with its "Enterprise in the Community" program. The facility holds pages on the worldwide register of professional services and employs full-time agents to help place new contracts for those at the end of existing contracts or for those who may be looking to step up their work commitments.

The jobs drift away to lower-cost areas has slowed to a trickle as most of the remaining service-intensive industries have not found it feasible to export jobs to lower-cost countries. Not only has it become apparent that physical presence is important in serving home markets, but that the need to couple knowledge-creation with delivery is the key to product development.

Hollywood content factories keep their creative teams closely tied to the company. Although production teams are spread wide from the Pacific to Europe, they work under the direct supervision of the feature director and are tied to long-term contracts of up to five years.

Although most companies have their enterprise information systems maintained and customized in Bangalore and Manila, most packaged software for the home and commercial market is conceived, designed, and constructed in the research labs of Menlo Park and Frankfurt. These software designers are some of the highest-paid individuals in the world. They are burnt out by the age of 30 as the companies employing them demand a high level of output to meet demands for new products to keep sales buoyant.

> **Software designers are some of the highest-paid individuals in the world.**

Insecurity about their ability to generate future income has led to a lack of commitment in the under-35 age group to purchase homes through long-term mortgages and loans. This has also required companies marketing savings and investments plans to offer schemes where the commitment to payment is spread over a shorter time frame when the client can be certain of an income.

Savings rates have increased as people save up to 50 percent of their income during periods of employment in order to insulate themselves from periods of inactivity or sabbaticals. Most people in the upper quartile of income have begun to take sabbaticals of approximately a year in duration. This will invariably involve undertaking an activity which will be a diversion from professional work commitments. Most popular is studying a new subject or deepening knowledge in an area of previous interest. Languages, earth studies, and the history of extinct cultures are the most common subjects taken. Much of this learning is done interactively via the variety of Virtual University services on offer. Other popular sabbatical pursuits include walking in remote mountain areas of Peru for the adventurous or hiking in the Himalayas for those who prefer the packaged comfort of Western-styled holidays.

> **People save up to 50 percent of their income during periods of employment.**

> **Frequent holiday sabbaticals have boomed in recent years.**

The majority of people working in "knowledge"-based jobs involving research, communication, finance, and the law work on short-term contracts or consultancy arrangements. They may frequently be working for more than one company at a time and are generally loath to turn down work, ending up working long hours and weekends to meet deadlines. No matter how successful, they never feel secure as individuals.

Some of these workers may have developed more entrepreneurial skills in selling their services and would begin to set up a hub or loosely formed association of fellow professionals who may not be quite as successful at selling themselves. The entrepreneur would typically refer work to those other associates and charge a fixing fee which may vary from 10–20 percent of the hourly rate. These networks or associations will be a continuously changing group as new members join whilst others leave to join new groups, and 80 percent of contracts will be with employers who they have worked for previously.

> *The massive move towards the privatization of welfare will ensure that employment in the insurance and the capital markets sector remains active.*

The employers who take on these temporary workers will generally be full-time employees who will be measured on their own effectiveness by the advice they obtain in executing their own job. Rather than being benevolent patrons they will be tough negotiators looking for value rather than prestige. They will themselves be generally busier than their contractors, spending more than half their time traveling away from the head office.

Most workers in service industries will have full-time roles and will be locally based. A substantial increase in those looking after the elderly will take place and wages for these workers will be at the low end of the wage scale. Strikes for more pay in this sector will be commonplace, but the workers will have difficulty getting public sympathy as most will regard their action as being unsociable and against old people who cannot fend for themselves.

The massive move towards the privatization of welfare will ensure that employment in the insurance and the capital markets sector remains active. Fund managers will be sought out more actively by companies and by private investors, with the major business publications publishing a regular "top ten" of the market's most favored fund managers.

Young people will be more employable the better educated they are. Graduates will compete with their peers from around the world and companies will seek applicants via the international recruitment pages of the Net. The key priority of the under-30s will be to work for a sustained spell with a large or medium-sized company to acquire core skills after graduating. These core skills will mold the direction of the individual's career for the rest of their life. The young that fail to achieve educationally would enter the physical services industries such as fast food, care for the elderly, and leisure. The few that show managerial talent in these early jobs may be promoted within those organizations to run larger units.

THE MID-LIFE ⧗ TIMES

January 2, 2015

Worldwide shortage of multimedia designers sends salaries sky high

More evidence that key employees are earning more than the CEO emerged last week in a recent survey of the multimedia industry.

The designers who package multimedia content for mass access on networks and on stand-alone devices are in short supply because of the hybridization of skills required to do the job.

The multimedia designer needs to be knowledgable in video production, sound editing, graphic design, journalism, and software engineering. Most educational qualifications only cover one or two of these specializations and the demands from the market have vastly exceeded the availability of individuals who are required to be these super hybrids.

Twenty-First Century Entertainments last week captured two of the finest designers from its rival, Global Dreamware, for an undisclosed sum believed to be in excess of $2.5m.

Karl Wehedhi, head of TFCE's multimedia design group, said, "The money is only good in so far as we feel valued. Our real motivation is in breaking new ground in the world of communications by merging art forms which have never before coexisted."

TELEWORKERS SUPPORT RAISES BANK'S PROFITS

Allied Banking Corporation's successful entry into offering teleworking services in local neighborhoods has helped contribute to over 20 percent of its profit at the half-year stage.

The bank, which charges a management fee for the use of office space and a range of specially designed support services, has benefited from the huge increase in people working within or close to their local communities.

Observers expect other banks to follow with similar services in the new year. "Our competitors have been waiting on the sidelines to see if customers will actually pay for services that they have previously provided at home. We have proved that there is an insatiable appetite for something which actually contributes to a sole trader's bottom line and actually saves a good deal of time."

Two die at strike-ridden home

Relatives of the two elderly residents of Park Gate Retirement Home who died last week expressed their horror at the callousness of the staff who have been staging their "work to rule" initiative for the last month.

The staff were protesting against the decision of management to limit wage rises to 2 percent for the third year in succession. They claim that care workers are one of the lowest-paid categories and yet require both physical and emotional commitment well beyond most other professions.

It is believed that the two fatalities were caused when workers failed to administer critical medication for the two people, who were suffering from a severe diabetic condition.

The Park Gate workers have now called off their strike as a mark of respect for the dead. A spokesperson for the group spoke critically of the management of the home, "The employers are holding us over a barrel. They are using emotional blackmail to blame any failure during industrial action on a lack of sympathy on our part."

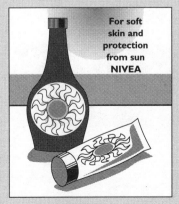

For soft skin and protection from sun **NIVEA**

Some of today's biggest brands are in anti-ageing products such as skin care creams. They also afford protection from the sun's ultra violet rays

■ The shrinking world

Travel

Air travel has seen sustained growth for the last two decades and now congestion in the skies is IATA's main concern. South-East Asian airlines account

Congestion in the skies is IATA's main concern.

for the majority of the world's largest carriers, with China Airlines having the greatest number of aircraft at 1,000. The Asian charter market is substantial, with 130 million Asians visiting Europe and North America every year. Top locations they visit are Paris, London, San Francisco, Orlando, and Toronto.

Open skies agreements have been operating in the West to varying degrees of compliance, and both China and India have been given until 2020 to join the agreement or face substantial curbs on their encroachment of world air routes. Open skies has resulted in the consolidation of Western airlines, and most small national airlines have all but disappeared. Two American airlines and one European now dominate airspace and there is aggressive competition for passengers on intercontinental routes.

Competition is not only on price but on service, reliability, and safety. Aircraft disembarkation has become a key source of competitive advantage for one airline, which has designed a unique seating configuration to allow every passenger to vacate a 400 seater in less than eight minutes from docking the aircraft. *Air Traveler* magazine carries independently audited league table ratings of punctuality, air safety, and disembarkation time.

Aircraft now fly in convoy guided by satellite Global Positioning Systems to maximize the use of time slots, and there is one air traffic control authority. The G70 nations took the decision to globalize their air traffic control after

Aircraft now fly in convoy guided by satellite Global Positioning Systems.

numerous incidents of strikes by national controllers caused untold disruption to world air travel.

Whilst air travel has boomed for long-distance, railways have made a comeback in most areas of the world for intracontinental travel. The greatest penetration of railways has been in the United States, where after 50 years of road and air travel, pollution and congestion have revitalized the railway system. In Europe too, most city center to city center journeys of under 500 miles are done by trains traveling up to 300 miles an hour. Sleeper services have been regenerated as executives are sold on the idea of combining travel with the needs for overnight accommodation. Efficient railway networks linking city centers across borders did most damage to the European airline industry, which had a generation earlier been sustained by price agreements on its short-haul continental routes.

Efficient railway networks linking city centers across borders did most damage to the European airline industry.

Meetings

Business people travel less now than they have ever done since the end of the last century. The significant improvements in video links and conference services have enabled most meetings to be conducted without leaving your desk at home or at the office. A busy executive's day is taken up mostly with back-to-back meetings held with up to three or four others in different locations. A mini camera fitted to a workstation transmits crystal clear images of the members involved in the meeting.

Corporations began to get concerned about the health of their top executives who seemed to spend 200–300 days a year away from their home location, mostly in aeroplanes. Concerns also extended to the productivity of these individuals who seemed forever caught up in airport lounges and transportation between the company's global locations. Today executives do meet face to face, but mainly for reasons when special protocol demands that they attend in person. This is usually for signing important joint ventures or for resolving areas of irresolvable conflict.

Most meetings to be conducted without leaving your desk at home or at the office.

Global brands

The Levitian dream is today's reality. Although there are many more global brands, there are an infinite number of variations to cater for local taste and preference. At least one Asian entrepreneur has successfully developed a chain of fast-food restaurants in Europe and North America. Oriental Express caters for the health-conscious snacker. Its food is low-fat, high-fibre, and contains aromatic spices in special Eastern concoctions. Hollywood film stars, popular musicians, and sports personalities have been used to promote the brand.

The Levitian dream is today's reality.

People are interested in the companies behind the brands they buy. Their top concerns are business ethics and environmental considerations. If a brand promotes goodness and wholesome ingredients then consumers will be keen to research and ensure that the claims are backed up. Any evidence that these claims are fabricated puts the company in grave danger of going under.

Some of the world's biggest brands employ independent ethics auditors to ensure that their codes of conduct are applied globally and that their annual financial accounts are accredited for ethical compliance. An ethical company is expected to treat its employees, suppliers, customers, and shareholders fairly. The closer a brand is to an ethical product, the greater the need for customers to feel that the company is ethical. Customers of a cigarette company would be less concerned by its medical ethics than say the customers of a bank or a waste management company.

In the mid-life scenario, brands are not valued for the status they provide but more for a symbol of quality and reliability. Customers constantly test these values in their purchases and do not rely on traditional loyalties. For example, branded software products are purchased for the bug-free, intuitive standards set by the manufacturer. Similarly, clothing is purchased for its durability, cars (in whatever form they exist) for the quality of their engineering and environmental compliance, and pension products for their stability and track record. The newly developed world, as in Asia, will consume Western brands as a symbol of attaining their new-found affluence very much along the lines of the way brands were built in the West in the latter half of the last century.

> Brands have also begun to fulfill a new role as an aid to selection in a sea of choice.

Brands have also begun to fulfill a new role as an aid to selection in a sea of choice. With the proliferation of products and services the consumer has begun to rely on established brands to reduce the field. Old-established brands that have maintained their original values for consumers will fare well.

Service has become an integral part of brand values. Advertising is just as likely to promote the service component of the offer as are its core features. Customers are just as interested in the service guarantees and continent-wide support for the digital notepads they purchase as they are in the storage capacity and interconnectivity. They fly airlines for reliability and ease of boarding, home shop for purchases because of the "no quibble" guarantee, and take vacations with operators who offer world class standards of comfort.

Global benchmarking

The shrinking world encourages people to compare products, services, and even the effectiveness of social and political systems around the world, more frequently and more critically. The pension program in Chile, the efficiency of the health system in New Zealand, the educational attainment with scarce resources of the children in China, and the community programs in Michigan will all be studied by countries in an effort to learn and improve their own systems. So customers also compare the time it takes to call out an engineer to fix the phone in New York, with that in London. They compare the quality of the French fries from McDonald's in Pittsburg with those in Paris. They contrast the check-in and check-out features of a car rental company in Denver with that in Delhi.

> They compare the quality of the French fries from McDonald's in Pittsburg with those in Paris.

Companies that supply global products and services will constantly monitor the standards of their products and services around the world. They even indulge in internal competitions to award prizes for the highest-achieving teams and in so doing constantly improve their own standards. The competition for being world class is unrelenting.

> The competition for being world class is unrelenting.

Communicating

What the fragmentation of communication channels did to destroy national mass marketing has been made up for by the global reach of television and other electronic media. The European Weather Channel is watched daily by ten million viewers, approximately the same number that would have watched a popular soap in Britain in the last century. Twenty-First Century Entertainment's Eco Channel has 30 million earthwatchers tune in worldwide to watch environmental updates every day.

English text in its simplest form can be recognized by nearly two billion people around the world. Most global advertising features simple, in-vogue English sound bytes, and digital information services on international networks are available mainly in English. An international style of English has begun to evolve which is free from idiom and metaphor. Its roots are in a global youth culture which borrows freely from great world languages.

> An international style of English has begun to evolve which is free from idiom and metaphor.

Sports and popular music are the two most universal forms of communication. Viewers watch mainly live concerts by megastars who invariably have their own record labels as the distribution costs have plummeted with the advent of digital call-down of albums on to domestic music systems. Most albums are co-packaged with video footage and some feature interviews with the stars during the making of the album.

The 2008 Olympics were watched by a record 3.4 billion people around the world simultaneously.

Sports features are beamed worldwide and nearly 90 percent of the audiences have never been to, or cannot afford, a real live fixture. Soccer still dominates for top viewing time, but increasingly viewers' interests are beginning to widen to a range of action-orientated sports, many of which have been designed and promoted specially for television. Channels have begun to specialize in one or two specific sports. There are, for example, ten soccer channels, two tennis channels, a golf channel, a winter sports channel, and several channels that feature events specific to a particular continent, such as North American sports. Successful sportsmen and women are used as icons of perseverance, health, and strength and are used to endorse goods.

> **Sports features are beamed worldwide and nearly 90 percent of the audiences have never been to, or cannot afford, a real live fixture.**

National backlash

> **The 30-year-old in Manhattan has more in common with his equivalent in Manila than with his 60-year-old father.**

Although in many areas the products are more global than they have ever been with commonalization of taste and preference, there has been an equal swing towards the need to preserve local and nation identity. Sometimes this has to be supported by law. Although people want to be associated with being international in their outlook, they are equally keen to preserve language, traditions, and culture. One hundred more countries have been created over the last 20 years.

Most of the need for national identity comes from the older generation, whilst the younger generation's preferences are of a more universal nature. The 30-year-old in Manhattan has more in common with his equivalent in Manila than with his 60-year-old father.

So dramatic has been the change in Asia that people have begun to be concerned by the change in moral values of the young. Children challenge the authority of their elders, teachers who once held sway over classes of 60 or more now have difficulty keeping order with half the number and religious leaders talk of an emerging generation of godless individuals.

> *Foreign companies are therefore faced with doing business in a politically fragmented subcontinent.*

In India some states have become so against the encroachment of multinationals and the profligate consumerism that is sweeping the subcontinent that they have put up insurmountable barriers to entry. People regularly march in protest against some major international corporation and burn or destroy its trademark or emblem to vent their anger. In contrast, other states court foreign companies for the investment and job creation they bring and are eager to compete for their capital and knowhow. Foreign companies are therefore faced with doing business in a politically fragmented subcontinent.

Asian visitors told to stagger coach parties to historic sites

Of the 100 million Asian tourists that visit Europe, many are drawn to the historic sites of which numerous legends have been told and around which several Hollywood films have been.

Now the biggest problem facing the Historic Sites Trust is managing the huge crowds that turn up and jam the tiny corridors and courtyards.

"They come over here and keep snapping away with their digital cameras for hours. After a while you have to tell them to move on or nobody will get a chance," said an usher at London's Abbey Road Studios, one of the most visited destinations in 2014.

A code of conduct is being issued to tour operators organizing trips for Asians. They include the following: keep groups to no more than 100; stagger visits by no less than 15 minutes; ensure each group stays no more than 5 minutes in any one location.

The Historic Buildings Trust has visited The Epcot Centre in Orlando, Florida, which holds the record of 50 million visitors a year, to study crowd control.

BUSINESS TRAVEL FALLS FOR THIRD YEAR RUNNING

Constant travel was once the main preoccupation of any international business person. It was also the major source of profitability for the world's airlines, which offered great incentives to their business customers to travel more rather than less.

Desktop videoconferencing has cut an executive's air-travel budget. Meetings are arranged back-to-back without leaving one's desk.

Gradually, with the introduction of personal video-conferencing and the enormous strides made in bandwidth availability, executives can drift effortlessly from one international meeting to another without leaving their desks.

Airlines have had to work hard to adapt to the fall in business travel and the increase in the leisure market. "Today it's either pop stars or punters," said one airline company representative.

Airline to withdraw safety pilots from air convoys

Five years ago when British American announced its air convoys to accommodate more of its airplanes to fit the shortage in time slots, observers were skeptical that passengers would buy into the safety issues associated with three aircraft flying together.

Last week it made one further leap into the future by announcing that only one of the three aircraft flying in formation would have a pilot.

Currently the air convoys have a safety pilot aboard each plane to allow for potential failures in the satellite Global Positioning Systems which guide each aircraft from take-off to landing.

Zero failure avionics have given the airline enough confidence to go ahead with the pilotless aircraft plan. Whether passengers will like the idea remains to be seen. So far, air convoys have not depleted the insatiable need for people to travel long distances.

Coca-Cola still at No. 1

The latest worldwide survey of the ten top brands people recognize still shows very little movement in the big brands of the 21st century.

Coca-Cola held the number one slot for the tenth year in succession. Its strong showing in Asian markets has helped keep it high in the charts.

A spokesperson for the company said, "This result does not surprise us. More and more people are drinking less alcohol, and for many consumers in Asia it is against their religion to take intoxicating drinks. Coke is a natural choice."

Coca-Cola is World Sports biggest sponsor. The television channel is distributed free on most domestic networks and is available worldwide. The channel boasts a viewing population of 35 million viewers under 24 years old.

■ The ascent of women

The female vote is largely behind the election of the first woman President of the United States of America. Her agenda is primarily to further the cause of equal opportunity for women in all walks of life. She is strongly in favor of introducing legislation to further reduce carbon emissions and to work with business to reduce the rising environmental burden being placed on subsequent generations. A strong advocate of "the woman's right to choose," she has campaigned for the need to make the once-a-year contraceptive freely available to all young women.

The female vote is largely behind the election of the first woman President of the United States of America.

The gap between women in senior management positions and their male counterparts has narrowed to a 40:60 split, yet only 10 percent of women have made it to CEO in the Fortune 500.

Sexual harassment cases are brought to the courts in 50 percent of cases by men. Generally men allege that they have been missed out on promotion because they did not respond to the advances of their female bosses. In most organizations, dating between the sexes is discouraged and anyone found to be doing so is given a disciplinary warning.

Sexual harassment cases are brought to the courts in 20 percent of cases by men.

Women in professional roles stay single till their middle-to-late '30s. Many never marry "because they could never find the time." Marriage is an ongoing "negotiation" between partners rather than a formal contract, and when the woman decides to have children she does so for the "experience." Maternity leave is usually for no more than six months and the children are cared for either by live-in parents or qualified childminders. The childminders often form a stronger attachment to the children in their early years than do their mothers.

Marriage is an ongoing "negotiation" between partners.

Women-only clubs, hotels, and restaurants are easily found and they are generally well patronized because they are seen as being "woman friendly." They assure not only privacy but physical security and many women may use these establishments as weekly accommodation to work in the city and save the daily commute to the suburbs.

Fashion and design for women are sober and conservative rather than extravagant and flashy. Women are more environmentally aware and take great care to ensure that the products they buy conform to some recognized

> *Few women eat red meat, and vegetarianism is twice as prevalent as in men.*

code of conduct. Generally products which have organic connections, and have been proven to enhance the health and care of one's person, are favored. Few women eat red meat, and vegetarianism is twice as prevalent as in men.

The Chinese leadership has taken a strong stand in encourageing women into government after thousands of years of women having had a repressed role. The Prime Minister asked women of China to be patient as changing a legacy of so many years could take time.

In India, more women now have a say in their marriage partner than at any time before, according to a survey on behalf of the *Hindustan Times*. The survey revealed that 70 percent of young women were in favor of their parents having a role as matchmakers but preferred the final choice of spouse to be theirs.

THE MID-LIFE ⧗ TIMES

January 4, 2015

Femina Hotels announces another bumper year

Femina Hotels, the chain established five years ago, announced another year of record profits. Occupancy of some of its newest hotels rose to 90 percent within a month of opening, according to its CEO, Kirsten Yeo.

The group plans to have a hotel in every major capital in Europe and seven new establishments in North America by the end of this year.

Femina was the brainchild of Yeo, who said that she felt, as a professional woman, uncomfortable in hotels when staying away from home.

"What I wanted was to come to a room with fresh flowers in a vase, with a bowl of fruit that I could help myself to, and other female company that I could talk to in the lounge in the evenings," she told *The Mid-Life Times* last year.

With the help of a business plan and a sympathetic venture capitalist, Anita Karlsberg, who shared the same views, she raised enough money to buy her first downtown Manhattan hotel. Subsequent hotels have replicated the same style of informality and home comforts.

The hotels have no more than 40 rooms, have health club facilities, a resident hairdresser and beautician, and all staff are women, with the exception of the security personnel.

Robochef targets working women

The days when women had to rush home from a day at the office, stick something in the microwave, and feed the kids may be over. Thanks to a new service launched last week by Robochef, a subsidiary of retail giant Safeburys, working mums can order from a weekly menu by phone, or via Intervision.

Ready-cooked food, kept warm in specially designed vans, is delivered to your door within 15 minutes of the appointed time of the order. There are over 50 options to choose from, including vegetarian and ethnic dishes.

All food carries a three-star rating by the famous Chinese chef James Wong. Its nutritional composition is approved by the Chief Medical Officer.

"After a week of using this service I cannot believe that I used to offer up such rubbish to my kids," said one mother. "I can now come home from work without the nagging guilt that I may not have anything left in the freezer or the bother of preparing a meal after a hard day's work. I suspect I'm paying about 10–20 percent over the cost of what I used to serve up. But it all seems to be worth it in terms of time saving and food quality. It's wonderful to know that we are eating the same food that the folks in that expensive restaurant are eating."

Robochef is aimed specifically at working women wth little time on their hands for shopping and cooking chores.

MEN SERVE WOMEN BETTER

A confidential study of customers carried out by British American Airlines found that women preferred male cabin crew. Stewardesses often tended to ignore their women passengers in favor of men, the survey revealed.

Women complained of feeling uncomfortable with the body language exhibited by female cabin crew. Men, on the other hand, were warm in their greeting and courteous in assisting women passengers to put away heavy luggage.

The airline is now incorporating these findings into its training program for all employees that have contact with customers. Trainers are making cabin crew more aware of "gender" in their dealings with customers.

Karlos Feldman, a leading women's fashion retailer, commenting on the survey, said, "We have always suspected that women feel uncomfortable serving other women. We tried an all-male team of shop assistants as an experiment in one of our fashion stores and found to our surprise that weekly sales jumped 55 percent almost instantly. Gender has got to be an issue in the buying decision."

Women's media channel popular with men

Viewing figures out this month show that a growing number of men are accessing the two most popular women's interactive multimedia magazines.

Both *Tara* and *Katia* reported a near 30 percent viewing population of men, up from 20 percent last year.

Women's on-line multimedia magazines have been slow onto the market because publishers believed that women as a group were not comfortable with the technology. Men's magazines have, on the other hand, been running successfully for many years. Women have been quicker in migrating from paper-format magazines than had been initially envisaged.

■ The privatization of welfare

Caring for the elderly

Care for the elderly is debated constantly in the media, in politics, and in the services sectors. The state has pulled out almost entirely from long-term provision for the elderly and throughout the Western world they are either accommodated within the extended family or on estates managed by construction-to-services companies.

Large areas of towns and principalities are dominated by the aged. They are usually in the more temperate parts of the world. In Europe, most of the Côte

> **The state has pulled out almost entirely from long-term provision for the elderly.**

d'Azur in France, Southern Andalusia in Spain, and the South-Eastern seaside resorts of Bournemouth, Eastbourne, and Brighton in Britain are given over to accommodating them. In the United States they spend their winters in condominiums in Florida and their summers in converted youth camps in Maine.

There are undoubtedly casualties amongst the old, where neither family, private sector, nor state can provide for them. They end up in senior citizens' dormitories run by the voluntary sector, or even worse in parks and pavements in crowded cities. Their plight has heightened awareness in the need for pension provision, and savings ratios in Western economies have begun to rise.

The elderly are serviced by younger, generally less educated workers who live in nearby estates and housing complexes. There is a growing resentment by them of the organizations that manage the institutions for the elderly. Pay and working conditions are generally at the heart of most grievances and sometimes this causes ill-feeling between the workers and their charges. The Union of Care Workers, one of the largest single unions, claims that 65 percent of all care workers are members.

Pensions and savings

The insurance companies have incorporated the plight of the unfortunate senior citizens into their advertising campaigns to encourage people to take out policies. They are supported by governments in trying to educate people to "save for their future." With the uncertainty that people face in their jobs, companies provide alternative mechanisms for savings to accommodate the variability in income.

Governments have been forced into considering strict regulation of the welfare insurance sector as they withdraw the existing safety net of state provision.

Managers of pension funds wield considerable clout with companies in which they invest, to the point that they have begun to dictate or validate corporate strategy. This has made top management more accountable to its shareholders and has weeded out non-performers. At the same time it has made strategies more conservative and less daring as the company CEO is aware that high-risk, high-reward ventures are not likely to find favor with investors.

The need to invest for the long-term has been been brought about by the privatization of welfare. The pursuit of quarterly results has given way to the long view. One of the three big accountancy firms has developed a set of accounting principles which provides the basis for the evaluation of the long-term viability of a company.

> *Governments have been forced into considering strict regulation of the welfare insurance sector as they withdraw the existing safety net of state provision.*

Health provision

Citizens are acutely aware of the cost of medical advice and treatment. Most countries have adopted the practice of the individual having to pay for medical treatment and recover the expenses from either the state system or via private insurance. There is a great deal of complexity and debate over the responsibility of state versus private systems.

The state tends to concentrate its resources on prevention, with a good deal of effort going into health education. Diet is an area most health educators have become concerned with as researchers have established that the majority of common ailments can be traced to poor dietary habits. The war on obesity and overweight is the primary cause for concern followed by the prevention of sexually transmitted diseases. Young people are encouraged to carry out regular screening for sexual diseases. The "clear" result is stored on the person's SmartHealth card. This sets off a trend in smutty jokes regarding SmartHealth cards.

The virtues of healthy eating are promulgated in the promotion literature of most packaged foods. Confectionery manufacturers have discovered zero-calorie chocolate

> *The state tends to concentrate its resources on prevention.*

> *Young people are encouraged to carry out regular screening for sexual diseases.*

candy, cereal suppliers stress the high-fibre content of breakfast cereals and fast-food retailers offer cholesterol-free hamburgers.

Cosmetic surgery has grown into a thriving industry as the over-65s wish to down-age their looks. The latest innovations in genetic technology are used to make their skin look like a 20-year-old's. Several surgeons are defending cases brought against them for operations that went wrong.

Uproar as Medilife introduces DNA tests

The medical and life insurance company Medilife was at the centre of a row last week when it announced that DNA tests would be introduced for all family-cover plans after January 1, 2015.

The family-cover plan is the company's special low-cost insurance plan for families with a good medical record. Medilife said that it had decided to introduce the tests after much discussion with family doctors and health industry experts.

DNA testing has trebled the cost of health insurance for some higher risk groups.

"It is our stated aim that we wish to keep down the cost of health insurance. These tests give us the best assessment we have ever had of a person's future health profile and thereby allow us to pass on the expected savings we would make over the life of the patient," said a spokesperson for the company.

Senior politicians were meeting last night to discuss the implications of this announcement. It has been the fear of many for some time that the insurers may introduce DNA testing as a device to discriminate against those with an unhealthy future. Some are also concerned that the DNA tests are equally accurate in predicting life expectancy and that this information could be used unfairly when estimating life insurance premiums for those people with long lives ahead of them.

SLOW CLAIMS PROCESSING IRKS PATIENTS

A recent survey of Medilife's customers has revealed that their number one complaint about the company is the time taken to process claims. Frequently the company will return forms if minor details have not been completed, adding to more delays.

Customers complain that the lengthy times for claims processing can result in funding problems for those undertaking expensive treatment. At least one bank has been offering bridging loans for those who need urgent surgery.

Another 500-unit estate for the elderly announced

The third major development for the aged has been announced in Restville, north of Nice on the Côte d'Azur. The development is part of the program of building 4,000 homes for the elderly by construction giant Surebuild.

Surebuild has almost exclusively focussed on the over-70s sector, since it was rescued from the brink of bankruptcy by Lifeassured, the European pensions company. Surebuild has engaged the well-known architect Alfred Heaney to design a complex which caters for the special needs of the elderly.

The complex has a 24-hour doctor-on-call facility, optional visiting meals-on-wheels, and several health and fitness rooms where the inhabitants can attend regular gym sessions.

Compulsory retirement at 70 called for

A spokesman for Jobs-for-Youth hit out last night at the disproportionate number of jobs being occupied by the over-70-year age group.

Unemployment in the 18–34 year-old category is three times that for the 55–70-year-olds that make themselves available for work. Employers appear to favor age and experience over youth. Increasing numbers of the senior age group have re-entered the work force, partly forced to do so by their underprovided pensions.

"We are not giving our young people a chance by giving jobs in preference to the old. The youth in our society have the energy and

vitality to make a major contribution, a fact which seems to have missed the employers who themselves are well past it," said the spokesperson. "We shall be calling for compulsory retirement of all those over 70."

The President of the troubled communications company Globalcomm, himself over 75, said, "Older people bring years of experience which the young can't hope to match. We believe in a balance of age, experience and the irrationality of youth."

Last year, Jobs-for-Youth and Schools-Before-Hospitals joined forces in a controversial campaign to legalize euthanasia.

■ Wired living

Digital technology has gradually spread throughout both the developed and newly industralized world, and more than 60 percent of people in Western Europe and North America live in homes that are wired to global information and communication networks. Some South-East Asian countries have an even higher proportion of wired households. In other parts of the newly developed world such as China and India, one-way multi-channel television is still the predominant communication medium as most of their modern telecommunication system has evolved via a cellular route.

> *The café or bar you go to after work will have the hottest game on general release that week.*

Most information is digitized and available on both private and public access networks. Intelligent Visual Presentation (IVP) devices, which display information and services in the home and in the office, are a mutation of the PC but with software resident on the network rather than on the display hardware. The cost of an IVP is less than a cheap suit, which makes it affordable in most rooms. IVPs are embedded into kitchen units, the side of a wardrobe unit in the bedroom, lie flat on the office desk, and may also be part of your head-up display in your car. The IVP in your doctor's surgery may subscribe to a medical information service, whilst the device in the waiting room of your hairdressing salon may have access to the latest top hairstyles. The café or bar you go to after work will have the hottest game on general release that week. With the software on the network the user only pays for what is being used.

> *Like the magazine evolved from the book, digital literature has evolved from the magazine.*

Digital literature (Digiture) is practiced as an art form. Like the magazine evolved from the book, digital literature has evolved from the magazine. Not only does digital literature accommodate the narrower field of vision available on an IVP, but its messages are concentrated into "communication bytes." Digital literature makes use of the powerful drill-down capabilities of the medium so that a story on, say, the nuclear terrorist incident in Tokyo can be accessed down a limitless hierarchy of detail. So if you only want to know the type of nuclear device being used by the terrorists, you don't have to read the whole article to find out. Digital literature also weaves in effortlessly the increased communication possibilities of sound and vision. Poetry is enjoying a renaissance because of its suitability

> *Wordsworth and Shelley are some of the most popular adaptations in digital literature.*

on this new medium. Wordsworth and Shelley are some of the most popular adaptations in digital literature.

Wired for service

IVPs provided by service companies provide specialized functions. The combined energy and water company has an IVP connected to your domestic metering equipment, through which you are sent bills for the energy you consume. Similarly banks have worked out that the next step up from the ATM outside the bank is the ATM (an IVP) in your home. Short of dispensing cash, the bank's IVP helps you transact all your banking business, pay bills, and recharge your electronic Smart card every time you leave home.

Similarly, mail order companies, grocery retailers, and entertainment companies want to provide you with an IVP if they believe that the volume of business you may transact with them will be significantly enhanced. Junk mail proliferates in our electronic mail boxes and companies offer expert systems to help weed out unwelcome mail. The traditional letter mail is expensive and is only used for more personal or low volume secure, guaranteed communications.

> *Junk mail proliferates in our electronic mail boxes.*

Quality and security assurance

Customers generally only buy products and services from companies that are members of the Wired Services Trade Organization (WSTO). The WSTO acts in a quality assurance role to ensure that its member companies trade ethically and deliver goods and services as described on their home pages. Numerous stories abound of how unethical traders have set up home pages to offer services, obtained money from unsuspecting customers, and closed down their operations within days. The WSTO seeks to protect customers from these occurrences.

Payment systems have been significantly enhanced in recent years by the advent of advanced encryption techniques and voice-pattern password recognition. When asked for her personal identification number, the payee speaks her digital password into a microphone integrated in the IVP. The voice patterns are matched with the bank's database and the transactions cleared.

The global market

As a supplier, being wired opens up your product to the world rather than a region limited by your salesforce or your advertising expenditure. This has been particularly dramatic for small suppliers of niche products and services. An economist specializing in forecasts of wood pulp supplies and prices, runs a multimillion dollar business making available his once-a-month forecasts worldwide. The 150 subscribers who pay $1,000 for each newsletter are from 35 countries around the world. A forecasting service which would previously only have been available to half a dozen users is now available worldwide.

> *As a supplier, being wired opens up your product to the world.*

A recruitment company requiring 40 PhDs in the history of language for a research program was able to acquire 60 top candidates for its client by placing the advertisements on their home pages. The candidates came from 34 countries.

Failed attempts at home shopping

Many retailers have attempted to run profitable ventures out of home shopping and failed. The customer seems happy to access home shopping services and browse, but does not buy expensive items or in any great volume. Analysts put this down to the significant number of customers who want to physically see and test out the products they buy. Also, shopping is both an entertainment and the chance to have physical interaction with others. There are exceptions, however. Discount houses that offer huge reductions on consumer durables and branded electronic goods prosper. Also minority groups that feel they are treated discourteously by shop attendants prefer the digital medium.

> *Many retailers have attempted to run profitable ventures out of home shopping and failed.*

Intranetworks

Most companies have their own communication networks, which utilize non-proprietary standards to enable open networking and interconnectivity. These networks support routine daily communication with workers around the world, knowhow exchange, and communication with suppliers and customers. The company intranet is protected by a multiple "firewall" of security systems to insulate it from unwanted intruders.

> *The open connectivity of these networks globally has brought customers, suppliers, joint-venture partners, and taxation authorities closer together.*

Physical and business mail and courier services are reserved only for remote locations of the world where company operations are still inhibited by poor telecommunications links. Some of the business mail services spawned in the last century have ended up maintaining and running company intranetworks and knowledge banks. The open connectivity of these networks globally has brought customers, suppliers, joint-venture partners, and taxation authorities closer together.

The virtual university

Three of the major business schools offer remote MBAs payable by subscription on the global network. Students register for courses and receive education by using interactive instruction on an IVP in their living room anywhere in the world. Students can learn at their own pace and take periodic short tests to validate learning as they proceed along a course of instruction. This avoids the need for a formal exam as marks are awarded continuously

Computer based interactive learning from an early age has paved the way to the development of the virtual university.

during the learning process. The leading business school awarded 350,000 MBAs last year and expects to treble that number by the end of the decade.

THE MID-LIFE ⧗ TIMES

January 6, 2015

Californians to vote digitally in next elections

Governor Sam Tan of California has announced that the next elections will be fought with digital technology. Electors will have the option of polling digitally or going to one of the polling booths on election day next summer.

Governor Tan said in a speech to the Electoral Reform Society, "There is an urgent need to revitalize the interest in the electorate to vote. More than 80 percent of our cititizens today are wired to public networks and this seemed a logical move."

Electors have already been campaigned heavily for the last two elections by prospective candidates for the state's top job. The cost of digital campaign literature is insignificant today, allowing most candidates the ability to put across their message effectively to millions of potential voters.

All voters will have to register their intentions to vote digitally by March 1 this year. They will receive an electronic voting form the day before election day and will have 48 hours to register their vote.

The move is being watched by other states which have a high percentage of users wired into Intelligent Visual Presentation devices.

More people read newspapers digitally now than on paper.

Homeshop Inc. in Chapter 11 disappointment

Homeshop Inc., the company with great hopes for a new age of digital home shoppers, announced that it would be filing for Chapter 11.

The company, which was launched in a blaze of publicity seven years ago, has been unable to finance its debt incurred in the expensive media campaign it undertook last year to revitalize flagging sales.

The CEO said in a statement to shareholders last year that the response to the campaign had been excellent, with the Homeshop Inc. shopping pages recording one million hits in a single day.

An industry analyst said last night, "One million hits probably didn't translate into many sales. The campaign merely served to arouse the curiosity of customers who called up Homeshop to browse rather than buy."

■ The fragile earth

A number of the islands in the South Pacific have been submerged.

Arresting the advance of global warming is society's greatest concern. Rising tides in coastal areas have begun to overcome barriers and the sea has laid claim to vast areas of low-lying land. The Maldives, once a thriving group of islands visited by tourists from Europe, lies with two-thirds of its mass submerged. Similarly, a number of the islands in the South Pacific have been submerged.

Freak weather seems to occur with some frequency, with high winds or torrential rain causing havoc with buildings and older structures that were not designed to withstand these extremes. Much of Venice has been given up to the elements, and London has regular flood warnings.

Much of Venice has been given up to the elements.

A decade ago most cities significantly curtailed the use of the gasoline-driven car and reduced much of the effects of asthma and low-level atmospheric pollution witnessed at the end of the last century. The inhabitants of inner cities are begining to vote for car-free estates and old city centres are being made car-free. It is quite unfashionable now to own a gasoline-driven car, and car-hire firms offer annual subscriptions to customers who want occasional access to a car. You can use a smart-key card to gain access to specially marked cars in parking lots. The distance traveled is logged to your account and you get billed monthly through your electronic bank account. The cars are all electrically powered and generally have a range of 150 miles before they are returned to a parking lot for recharging.

It is quite unfashionable now to own a gasoline-driven car.

The newly industrialized economies have fought hard to maintain their right to use carbon-emitting fuels for another ten years as they engage in a program of implementing renewable sources of energy. Trade sanctions are the greatest pressure that the old developed countries use to get agreement on the curtailment of carbon emissions.

Business and the environment

Business and the environment has become a catch-all phrase for the ability of companies to work in a way that is sympathetic to environmental concerns. Consumer pressure has been the greatest way to get companies to work within standards set down by the Environmental Protection Consortium (EPC). These cover codes of ethics for waste management, packageing of products, energy management, and even the engagement of personnel

The train makes a comeback after rising concern about carbon emission from cars and extreme traffic congestion.

as policemen to oversee the observance of these standards.

The EPC is a global organization, jointly funded by the world's 100 largest companies and based in Singapore. It agrees standards and promulgates new versions which can be accessed via its home pages on the net. Its consultancy services are sought by many companies that wish to comply with the standards and obtain the annual EPC audit certification. Two of the largest financial auditing firms have links with the EPC and their auditors are approved to certify companies. This certification is issued as a "permit to operate" in many countries and is published at the end of the financial year, together with the financial accounts.

Companies have sought to use these standards not only as a means of achieving compliance but also to improve the efficiency of waste management and to improve manufacturing yields. Water companies have found it more efficient to reduce leakage in pipework than to build more processing plant; petroleum companies that previously flared off gas find it more efficient to use for power generation; and a drinking soda manufacturer has discovered that recyclable containers are not only a hit with its customers but that they have reduced the cost of packaging.

> The US has set a new target to reduce its per capita waste down to 1,000 pounds from an all-time high of 1,700 ten years ago.

The US has set a new target to reduce its per capita waste down to 1,000 pounds from an all-time high of 1,700 ten years ago. This was brought about by an extreme shortage of land-fill sites, amid mounting opposition from the communities where new sites were being proposed. Europe too, having fewer land-fill sites to choose from, has cut back per capita waste to 500 pounds. Strict penalties are imposed on companies that exceed packageing levels set down by the Environmental Protection Consortium.

Manhattan votes for 9–5 car ban

In a surprise vote last week, the inhabitants of Manhattan, taking part in the first major digital referendum in the US, voted for a ban on the gasoline-driven car between the hours of 9am and 5pm.

The vote was brought about by the new mayor, Harry Strognoffsky, who campaigned to find a solution to the rising toll of pollution-related breathing disorders in the city's population. "No longer can we sit idly by and watch our city choke to death," he told a Manhattan inaugural luncheon.

Business people received the news with mixed views. Some spoke of the impracticalities of the ban, bearing in mind the lack of an appropriate transport infrastructure, whilst others welcomed the result as a vote for common sense.

If approved, the ban would apply to all gasoline-driven cars between the peak commercial hours of the city. Electric cars would be allowed to operate and the many taxis which are now driven by electricity would be the major beneficiaries.

Gasoline-electric hybrids would also be allowed under the ban, provided they continue to drive with electric traction.

New York pollution levels rise to an all time high resulting in an automobile ban.

Garbage theft on the increase again

The garbage theft that stopped two years ago is back on the increase again according to new statistics released today.

The Metropolitan police chief said he would be stepping up security patrols of the U47 garbage depot, particularly at night, when most of the thefts have occurred.

Metropolitan Recyclers, the company which owns the depot, reported losing $10 million in recyclable waste from the depot last year. Aluminum, paper, and magnetic ferrous material were the most popular with thieves.

Customers boycott Indonesian furniture

Customers have staged demonstrations outside the Indonesian furniture retailer Woodcraft for the third week running. They are protesting at what they describe as the unnecessary mass destruction of one of the few remaining rain forests in the world.

Woodcraft has made a virtue out of the traditional craftsmanship of its furniture and the quality of the solid teak of which it is made. A spokesperson for the company said, "We are just as concerned as these protesters about the state of our forests and we do put back what we take away. We have a program of replanting new saplings and managing thousands of hectares of land which are in the process of being regenerated and handed back to native peoples."

A representative of The Campaign for the Preservation of Rain Forests told *Mid-Life*, "Solid teak furniture from these ancient forests is about as socially correct as wearing mink was early this century. We think the use of solid wood to construct these tables, chairs, and cabinets is unnecessary when we have so many alternative materials around these days."

AIR AND WATER ANALYZER MOST POPULAR GIFT THIS CHRISTMAS

An $18.50 analyzer which tells you if the air you're breathing or the water you want to drink is safe set all records as the gift that most people will see in their Christmas stocking this year.

Earth Products, the company that markets the electronic device, said that it has a range of other environmental devices in the pipeline. "The Essential Analyzer was devised in our Palo Alto labs in response to global opinion research we conducted. It showed that people the world over are most concerned with the possible harm being done to them by pollution in the essentials of life – air and water," said Director of Research, Melita Nally.

The company is planning to introduce an additive analyzer this spring. It produces information on the additive content in packaged foods and indicates where levels may be above international standards.

French nuclear decommissioning debate continues

The European Union was calling for a published program of decommissioning for six French nuclear-powered stations, which are now over 35 years old and at the end of their design life.

Électricité Européen, the engineering-to-power company, has said that its engineers have given the installations another five years of "fitness for purpose" and that the proposed $15 billion decommissioning program will not now commence until 2020.

The announcement has infuriated Euro Ministers from Germany and Britain who say they have another Chernobyl on their hands. They will be taking the matter to the European Court in Strasbourg.

■ The globalization of politics

> *A balance of power exists between the politicians, business people, and single-issue-based communities.*

Few nations today could claim to be autonomous in the important decisions they make with regard to taxation, welfare, defense, or the general running of the economy. A balance of power exists between the politicians, business people, and single-issue-based communities of interest. As a result, change is slow, and despite politicians sometimes winning near-landslide victories at the polls, any significant change in direction is reacted to swiftly by the financial markets or issue-based community action.

The total volume of traded stock is more than ten times the combined GNP of the world. Although currency trading has fallen with convergence to a single currency, in three of the world's biggest markets, foreign exchange dealers have been able to precipitate the fall of weak governments in at least two instances in the last ten years.

> *There is constant talk of the need for real moral leadership in politics, but few politicians can stand up to such ideals.*

In Western economies the percentage of those who vote has fallen consistently because voters have become more apathetic about the role of politics. There is constant talk of the need for real moral leadership in politics, but few politicians can stand up to such ideals. Fear of physical safety and the lack of a private life are the greatest deterrents for people with political ambitions.

Both the newly industrialized countries and the developing ones continue to be governed by an ever-ageing group of leaders. The Western-styled democratic process is considered to be inappropriate by its leaders and, with a few exceptions, the process of government continues unchanged.

> *Political parties have formed consortia with other parties within their trading block and beyond.*

Political parties have formed consortia with other parties within their trading bloc and beyond. These federated political parties have begun to behave like global corporations, sharing research and education programs and developing joint policies to implement around the world. This is perhaps the most significant threat to international companies that might change the existing balance of power.

Nationalism

With a background of federalism and trading blocks we have an enhanced sense of nationalism, traditional roots, and culture. Old, extinct languages are being reinstituted into schools, and politicians stand for election on nationalistic platforms. In Wales and Ireland more people speak Welsh and Gaelic respectively as a first language than English, and in Brittany Breton predominates over French. In the US, Spanish vies closely with English and it is fashionable for second or third generation immigrants in North America to retrospectively learn the language of their forefathers.

Companies are keen to promote the national origins of the components of a product when it is being sold in that country. An airline promotion in Britain may stress the quietness of the Rolls-Royce engines, in France it will stress the cooking by a top French chef, in Singapore the standards of service by its Asian cabin crew, and in the US the tradition of Hollywood on its entertainments channels.

Single-issue politics

Global communities sharing common causes have organized themselves around single issues, usually when frustrated by the interest shown by traditional politicians. Several issue-based communities exist based on environmental issues such as carbon-emitting plant, machinery and automobiles, protection of wildlife and the countryside, and the management of waste. Animal rights activists have supporters across the Western world, whilst human rights groups have wide-ranging membership across the whole world.

> *These single-issue groups use consumer activism as their major weapon .*

These single-issue groups use consumer activism as their major weapon to oppose companies that are seen to be breaking their code. They use the Net as a means of spreading news of boycotts, and their action can be felt by global corporations within a few hours. Most corporations have liaison officers whose job it is to keep contact lines open with the most powerful of these groups. Many corporations have sought to co-operate with these groups and involve their most influential leaders in relevant discussions.

These groups have loyal supporters and they use devices such as the affinity card, in alliance with certain banks, to collect subscriptions to fund their activities. They organize summer camps for members and their families, where they have the chance of getting together. Generally their activities in connection with their common cause are executed mainly through cyberspace.

Business lobbying

Businesses have external relationship divisions which focus their efforts on identifying single-issue communities and establishing which groups could have the greatest influence on their business. Those that are the most organized and most passionate about their cause are given the greatest attention. Current business ethics codes dictate that a company should trade in a way that is not harmful to the environment or the community. Businesses that have declared themselves to be "ethical" explain to outsiders how they comply with the standards.

Businesses complain of the blackmail and cheap publicity tactics used by some of the campaigners, and the relationship between the two groups is often the subject of some acrimony.

THE
MID-LIFE ⧗ TIMES

January 8, 2015

Earthwatch affinity cards break all records

In a world of proliferating affinity payment cards, the Intersmart organization published last week the top 20 global affinity cards it now supports.

The Earthwatch card was notable for its significant lead over other rivals such as the IWA, the International Weapons Association, and the ANL, the Animal Rights League.

."Our card has been a great success," said Sharuna Sharma, the organization's finance officer. "We have a 100 percent acceptance of our cards which members receive on joining Earthwatch. Over 65 percent of those members are active users of the card."

Funds raised from the card are used to finance Earthwatch's high-profile environmental awareness campaigns. Last year its support of the Democratic Alliance Party was orchestrated through a major poster campaign, paid for by Earthwatch and featuring the slogan "The party that will create a future for our children."

Dealers bring government to point of collapse

The government of Punjab was in crisis last night after the money markets triggered a collapse of the Rupya, due to a leaked report suggesting that the introduction of currency controls might be imminent.

John Detwyler, head of money markets at Deutche Ramen & Willard, said, "We have been unhappy for some time with the fiscal policies of Punjab's chancellor, Kirpal Singh. These leaked reports have confirmed our fears."

Ever since its secession from India, the Freedom Party has struggled to keep inflation down in an economy which has not been able to attract enough of its expected émigrés, which it had hoped for to revitalize the economy.

GLOBAL ALLIANCE AGREES TO ENVIRONMENTAL AGENDA

The global alliance of Progressive Social Reform parties met for their annual conference in Tashkent last week, the third so far.

This, the biggest alliance of left-of-centre parties, has representation from 32 countries around the world, including Germany, Britain, France, the United States, and Argentina.

The conference debated the need for a global environmental agenda, the content of which included the controversial carbon tax, which was originally promoted by the United States.

Leaders agreed to adopt the environmental code and incorporate it into their own national manifestoes.

Singapore announced the development of its tenth satellite city in Myanmar. Clones of Singapore exist all over Asia.

The two-tier world (I'm alright) scenario

Summary

In this scenario the world is split further into the "alrights" and the "lo-eds." Alrights are highly educated and work in the knowledge-intensive industries, while the lo-eds are poorly educated and work in service industries. The United States and Europe develop their own two-tier societies with a widening gap between rich and poor. State subsidies to rescue the unfortunate from the poverty trap will have diminished, taxation at source will be considered unfashionable, and most health systems will have been privatized. Asia and South America too have their two-tier societies, for although these regions will grow enormously in wealth, there will be a continuing divide between rich and poor. The favellas of Rio and the gated estates of Los Angeles replicate themselves around the world. In this scenario, market segmentation according to Maslow is more appropriate than Neilsen or Acorn. We have people with basic needs such as food, shelter, clothing, transportation, and clean water, and people with higher needs such as discovery, belonging, travel, and security.

■ The family

The family today has changed out of all recognition to what it was last century. Fewer than 20 percent of children are together with their natural parents by the age of 16 and temporary cohabitation has replaced marriage as the primary institution by which couples live together.

Alrights, who form 10 percent of the population, and the rest, the lo-eds, follow similar patterns of family behavior. Alrights, however, enter into formal legal contracts with their cohabitees to ensure against future claims when the relationship breaks down. With lo-eds, cohabitation is a more informal affair as they tend to live on a more day-to-day basis without the encumbrance of personal assets, often driven by the need to afford shelter.

Sixty percent of lo-ed mothers have children under the age of 20 and end up having to look after the children on their own. If these young mothers happen to find work in one of the many low-paid service industries, then virtually all their income is consumed in paying for cheap accommodation and basic food. Most lo-ed mothers are emulating the experiences of their own mothers, who became grandparents before the age of 40.

Although China is today the world's biggest economy, 400 million people earn less than $800 per annum.

Lo-ed children are left to fend for themselves for most of the day whilst their parents are out at work. The sight of young children playing in a decaying London street with its backdrop of old Victorian housing resembles a scene from a Dickensian novel. More than half the children play truant at least once a week, and the education authorities have long given up the idea of enforcing school attendance.

Most state-run schools fulfill the role of young person's refuge rather than a place of learning. Children are let into school after body searches at the gate by armed guards. The school is then sealed off to outsiders until the afternoon when the inmates are allowed to go home. Teaching is continually disrupted by unruly pupils who frequently use violence against teachers and other students caught up in gang warfare.

Lo-ed families live on housing estates which have been built in the last century. The building stock is rundown and most of the infrastructure of roads, sewers, and street lighting is in a state of continual disrepair. Some estates have arisen on demolished waste land with "Iggies," extruded metaloplastic dome-shaped, one-roomed homes packed in rows: the 21st-century equivalent of cardboard city.

> **The only trading activity conducted is in car-trunk sales.**

Most of these estates are no-go areas for alrights, and police do not guarantee the safety of individuals who enter these areas without cover. Doctors on call, maintenance crews, and other services are usually given police protection when they enter these "unsafe" areas. No retail shops or banks exist in the vicinity of these areas and its inhabitants have to travel long distances to reach shopping areas. The only trading activity conducted is in car-trunk sales, where lo-eds bring stolen items to trade.

There are shopping areas which are specially designed for low-eds, where the value proposition is dominant. Alright children refer to their low-ed counterparts as the *savvy* kids, after the name of a supermarket chain which specializes in discount packaged foods that have passed their sell-by date.

> **Alright children refer to their low-ed counterparts as the savvy kids, after the name of a supermarket chain.**

Alright families shop in specially guarded shopping malls which are one of the few places where you can browse around the shops freely without fear of being attacked and having your Intersmart payment card stolen. Shop Till 'U Drop (STUD) malls, the most successful this decade, exclude low-eds to protect their affluent clientele by barring anyone who does not have a gold or silver level Intersmart card.

Alright couples usually meet and decide to cohabit while at university or immediately thereafter. If they have not found a partner, then they will seek the services of an introduction agency later in their 30s. The introduction agency's search for a partner often extends across national boundaries: Colombia and the Philippines have become particularly popular with Western males looking for hausfraus.

> **Neighborhoods are usually patrolled by private security firms.**

Alright families have at least one full-time domestic worker who lives-in on the premises. Households may have several part-time *domestics* who work on different days of the week for other families in the neighborhood. These neighborhoods are usually patrolled by private security firms and in some cases, completely fenced off as a protection against crime. Lo-eds are only allowed into these areas if they are domestics or involved in service deliveries.

Insurance companies have begun to encourage alrights to employ security patrols in addition to the electronic protection mechanisms that are now de rigueur. New housing complexes for alrights are now invariably gated and the property companies promote the resulting low insurance premiums as a special feature.

At least 100 countries in the world are bankrupt, their citizens live in extreme poverty.

The DOUBLE STANDARD

January 1, 2015

O'Mally Homes are "safer than houses"

The building company O'Mally Homes announced that its new range of up-market family homes was the safest house that anyone could buy today for under half a million dollars.

The newly designed homes are part of a refocussing of the company's operations on those looking for security in these crime-ridden times. A company spokesperson for O'Mally said, "Market research has told us that safety from burglary and violence is the major concern for knowledge professionals. These homes have been designed to be impregnable to external intrusion by undesirables."

The homes are clustered in groups of 12 with high-voltage protection wire ringing the 12-foot walls which surround each mini-estate. The entrance gate is operated by a remote controller fitted to a car. At night an armed guard occupies the gate-house as added protection, and each house is fitted with an emergency alarm connected to the local rapid-deployment police center.

Most of O'Mally's new homes have been sold before a single brick has been laid.

Savvy supermarkets act to cut shrinkage

Last year the Savvy supermarket chain lost 15 percent of its stock through shrinkage, which its CEO, Harry Johnson, said would "bust the company." Today Johnson and his managers are fighting back with an aggressive plan to combat the light-fingered customers and workers.

Savvy is taking a step back in time to the days when shopping assistants served people from behind a counter. Customers asked for what they wanted and were handed the items requested upon payment.

Customers will be able to browse through the entire range of products on display, with dummy products on show. The cans of baked beans will be empty, loaves of bread will be made of plastic look-alike material, and meat will be sprayed with a formaldehyde to render it inedible.

Customers will tick their orders on special order forms and hand them to the sales assistants who will then pack the items requested. When payment has been made, the customers will be ble to collect their goods from a collection kiosk.

Savvy hopes that the plan will cut shrinkage and improve profitability. Although the initiative will increase costs, with labor at $2 an hour it could recover its investment in a few weeks with shrinkage being reduced by 80 percent.

STUD MALLS A CRIME-FREE HIT

The Shop Till 'U Drop malls have been pulling in record numbers of shoppers this Christmas due to its ingenious way of cutting crime in our shopping centres.

To visit the STUD malls you have to insert a gold or silver Intersmart payment card to get through the entrance. One hundred smart-points are awarded to every first-time visitor and 50 points for every subsequent visit.

A spokesperson for the STUD Development Company said, "Our malls are appealing to the top 5 percent of the population, who wish to spend their hard earned income in a quality, trouble-free, crime-free environment. With the record of theft and physical violence to high-net-worth individuals in our city-based shopping centers, STUD is the only safe alternative."

The malls feature a range of entertainment facilities, a top restaurant, a cinema, and franchise retail outlets operated by the world's most famous brand names.

Family Protection Corp hit by scandal

The Family Protection Corporation has been alleged to employ illegal aliens in its personal protection unit. In view of the national security implications of significant numbers of these individuals, who possess arms in connection with their protection duties, an injunction has been issued for FPC to cease trading until it has been cleared of these allegations.

No one was available yesterday at the Cayman Island registered company for comment.

The Family Protection Company has provided armed bodyguards for wealthy businessmen and their families over the last five years and has grown into an international business with a turnover of $150 million.

■ The breakdown of welfare

Crime

Lo-eds have little to fall back on when they are unable to find work or when they suffer an illness. Most turn to crime as a means of making an income when it is difficult to find employment. The authorities have accepted that large urban areas are unpoliceable and have embarked on a strategy of keeping crime out rather than locking up criminals. The prison population is both unmanageable and unaffordable and the existing prison accommodation is now reserved specifically for political or serious mentally unstable prisoners.

> *The authorities have accepted that large urban areas are unpoliceable.*

When alrights venture out of their crime-free zones they do so at some risk. Bullet-proof, secure cars are necessary, and in the event of breakdown the driver and occupants are advised to stay in their locked car and call for help on the cellular telephone. Breakdown services are themselves armed to ward off potential attackers.

> *Physical security is an individual's primary concern.*

Physical security is an individual's primary concern and attacks get more blatant and frequent every day. Theft is the most frequent cause of these attacks.

Health

The average life expectancy in most Western countries has fallen for the first time in 100 years. Infant mortality is the greatest casualty, and post-natal treatment is non-existent for lo-eds. Top killers are heart disease caused by coronary disorders and this can usually be traced to an unhealthy diet, high in animal fats. Overweight and obesity are common, mainly due to a nutritional imbalance high in sugar and starch. Smoking-related cancer is another cause of death, and many lo-eds now buy cigarettes by the stick rather than by the packet full.

> *The elderly have been hit hardest. Many have to work well into old age to pay for life's basics.*

Private sector treatment is unaffordable for lo-eds and health insurers would identify them as being the highest at risk from ill-health due to poor housing and diet. Health provision for the lo-eds is non-existent other than the support given by a few charitable institutions funded by sponsored lotteries.

Alrights by contrast go to expensive health clubs, seldom smoke, and are more cautious of their nutritional intake. Many strive to keep down their weight, not by exercise but by liposuction. And "weight reduction" surgeries have sprung up all around the Western world, with Miami and Nice, on the French Riviera, being the world's centers for this expertise.

The world has left Africa on its own to combat the unrelenting spread of Aids and other killer diseases. The combination of population explosion and lack of resources has set health and economic progress back 50 years. The average life expectancy is 27, the lowest in the world, and Africans traveling abroad are subject to extensive health checks before gaining entry to countries in the Northern hemisphere. Aircraft that fly in and out of the most infectious countries in Africa are fumigated and sterilized in special quarantined areas before being allowed into the general aircraft-handling terminals.

> *Aircraft that fly in and out of the most infectious countries in Africa are fumigated and sterilized in special quarantined areas.*

Uncared-for elderly

The elderly who lived through the boom in state welfare last century and did not provide for an alternative means of old-age welfare are hardest hit in today's world of "I'm alright." Many of them live in makeshift housing and have had to find jobs at abysmally low wages to pay for life's basics. They have either pawned or bartered most of their few precious belongings to raise cash, and they may often be found outside shopping malls or in church halls on Saturdays selling their last few possesions.

> *Every week there are stories of private pension funds collapsing in an unregulated market.*

Alrights who had the economic means to provide for old age, although comfortably off, are increasingly wary of the future security of their funds. Every week there are stories of private pension funds collapsing in an unregulated market, and governments have done little to regulate the governance of these funds.

Granalot offers punters big wins

Granalot, the new lottery aimed at subsidizing hospitals for the elderly, was launched this week. The organizers promised that the top prizes for the winners would surpass everyone's expectations.

Lottery payouts have been falling in recent years as several charities have sought this device as a means of raising funds. "Most low-waged or un-waged people have a limited amount of capacity for gambling. The plethora of lotteries that have sprung up are competing for a limited amount of available cash," said a spokesperson for Gamblers Anonymous.

The organizers of Granalot said that they were able to increase the size of their payouts by minimizing the amount spent on administration. Whereas most other charities use agents to administer their lotteries, Granalot is organized directly, using technological innovation.

More than half the income each week is passed on as prize money, compared with less than 25 percent in the other competing lotteries.

Granalot's big-prize payout

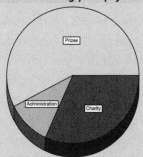

Prizes
Administration
Charity

Gambling is now the world's biggest industry. "Lo-eds" dream of big wins to assure their long-term security.

New killer virus heads West

Deng fever attacks the old and vulnerable and kills within 24 hours of taking hold of the body's immune systems.

It has been responsible for wiping out the elderly populations of many villages in China's Guandong province. Doctors are referring to it as the most age-selective virus ever known to man.

Researchers at the Institute of Tropical Medicine have been working around the clock to find an inhibitor to the virus, which has begun to attack communities in North Africa and the Middle East.

Airports in all Western capitals were on alert for the killer virus. Flights from infected areas were being refused landing permission, and all aircraft flying to and from Asia and Africa were being fumigated in special quarantined areas. Anyone over the age of 60 on board these flights was required to spend 24 hours in detention centers before being allowed to enter the country.

New liposuction technique promises weight loss on demand

A new technique for liposuction developed at the Medical Research Laboratories of AlfaFactors in Miami claims up to 25 percent weight loss can be achieved in hours.

The new technique removes fatty tissue, which traditionally builds up around the hips, stomach and chin, without the need for anesthetics. Doctors claim that the $7,500 treatment can be administered as frequently as a person wishes.

"People who put on weight through excessive eating or who have a predeliction to putting on weight need not have to worry any more about what or how much they eat," said doctor Aneka Pryke at her surgery in West Keys, Florida.

Infant milk producer expands distribution

Infanurse, the Swiss-based, infant milk production and distribution company announced record profits following the introduction of its new colostrum-rich product lines.

"Our new product line is the result of a decade of research to reproduce as closely as we can a mother's milk output," said a spokesperson for the company. "Working mothers today cannot afford the luxury of staying at home to breast feed their children. We have the right products to allow them to get back to work as soon as possible."

Infanurse has in the past been criticized by doctors for claiming that substitute milk was better for babies than their mother's milk. The company appears to have abandoned this stance in favor of stressing the convenience and freedom that infant milk substitutes bring to working mothers.

Infanurse's biggest markets are currently in Africa and Asia.

■ Jobs

Jobs fall into two broad categories: professional and services. Alrights usually have highly paid professional jobs, whilst lo-eds have jobs in the low-paid service industries. Many of the skill-based, managerial, and administrative jobs were automated over the last 20 years, or eliminated because they were considered unnecessary. A small percentage of people have dropped out altogether from society and carry out an alternative lifestyle in the low-skilled cottage-based craft industries.

Alrights benefit from a high standard of education provided through expensive private schooling and equally expensive colleges and universities. The new breed of professional is called a knowledge worker and spends between 12 and 15 hours a day at work. The professional's expertise is in accessing knowledge speedily, processing it, and then acting upon it or recommending actions to his or her employers.

Good investment advice is the top concern for those with money. As a consequence, financial advisers and fund managers together with tax consultants command high salaries, usually working as self-employed consultants. Both lawyers and doctors have effectively managed to regulate entry into their professions and maintained their place at the table of high earners.

> **Good investment advice is the top concern for those with money.**

Lo-eds lack the educational attainment to take on knowledge-intensive jobs and end up in the low-skilled service jobs in retailing, food preparation, distribution, and domestic work. The average rate per hour for service jobs is a fraction of that commanded by the professions, and service workers often have more than one job to make a reasonable income. A worker may work by night for a security firm and spend the day working in a fast-food restaurant.

The DOUBLE STANDARD

January 3, 2015

Literacy rates the lowest this century

When Bill Keanu, manager of a convenience food restaurant, discovered that half his staff could not read, he decided to send them on an adult literacy course which he partly funded.

Bill's experience is backed up by a survey out today which shows that literacy rates are now the lowest they have been since records were kept.

"School class sizes are so unmanageable now that teachers cannot provide individual coaching or detect serious learning weaknesses," said a senior schools inspector yesterday. Combine that with 280 television channels to choose from in the home and you get major disruption and change in a child's learning program.

It is common to see a chalked sign outside a butcher's shop with misspellings and grammatical errors.

Keanu first spotted the problem when he asked a member of staff to read the new company procedures on safety and found that fewer than 50 percent of the staff had been able to read it.

Now many managers like him are looking to adopt similar education schemes in an effort to solve the chronic shortage of staff at affordable levels of salary.

Firms looking at hiring professionals from abroad

The search for top professional managers is ending in a dead end for many companies looking to hire professionals in key areas of international management. They are therefore looking at the overseas market to attract the best brains.

"The world gives us a bigger base from which to draw," says Carla Timpson, the director of human capital at Smith, Roderick and Rees, the financial advice firm. "Our own educational institutions are having to draw from a smaller base of academically superior pupils every year. As a consequence, fewer good-quality candidates come through on leaving university."

STRIKE AND INDUSTRIAL SABOTAGE RECORD WORSENS

Unofficial and wildcat strikes have been rising despite shrinking trade union membership amongst the workforce.

A survey out today revealed that since the turn of the century trade union membership has dwindled to less than 50 percent. In spite of this, strikes have increased.

Doug Mountjoy, head of employment policy studies, said, "Our service industries are today in the hands of workers who have shallow skills and can be replaced by others if need be. However, workers can do enormous damage in a short campaign before the management can find replacement workers."

"Drivers can bring critical supply chains to a halt in remote areas by walking off and leaving their vehicles. Employees can pass on critical passwords to computer systems and disgruntled food workers can do irreparable damage to a company's reputation."

183

PART FOUR

HOW TO DEVELOP SCENARIOS

T his is how we look at developing scenarios in this chapter:

- *The guiding principles of inclusion, universality, and poignancy*

- *The steps to scenario development*
     Choosing the area of investigation
     Establishing the vectors of change
     Preparing the team
     Developing and presenting antithetical outcomes
         The key ingredients of an outcome
         The results
         Products and services needed
     Identifying scenarios via common themes

- *Applying the scenarios*
     Testing your existing strategy
     As an innovation engine
     Scenario milestones
     Consulting the oracle – using scenarios to make decisions

The three ingredients for success

There are three guiding principles in developing scenarios; Inclusion, universality, and poignancy. We shall examine the relevance of these in turn.

Inclusion

The success of scenario planning is in the eyes of those who participate in the exercise rather than the elegance of the output. It is at its most powerful when used as a process of getting a group to build consensus and understand the underlying reasons for embarking on a strategy. All those involved should feel included.

In my early research on scenario planning I interviewed some of the members of the Shell scenario planning teams who have since contributed to spreading the use of the technique in companies around the world. Professor Kees Van der Heijden tells of the way Shell managers would gradually converge on a consensus on the implications of a decision by being able to participate in developing the various outcomes of the forces of change relevant to their business.

DeAnne Julius, British Airways' chief economist, tells of the way the airline's executives were able to track the implications of the fall in the numbers of "conspicuous" consumers and the rise in the "individuated" consumer. What would the "individuated" consumer want of British Airways in the future – would they travel more or less frequently, what levels of service would they demand, and how could the airline meet their needs?

When a group generates scenarios it is translating facts and intuition into an amalgam of the way its business might look in the future. The debate and the discussion are often more important than the result. An outsider to the group may often find scenarios quite uninspiring and unremarkable.

Three ingredients for scenarios

Inclusion – Involve all those
who need to own the decision

Universality – Research
all shades of opinion

Poignancy – Re-create the
scenarios vividly

Universality

The wider the initial search for forces of change the richer the material you will have to play with. Take in and respect all views, no matter how much you may disagree with them. The more you listen to unconventional views the more likely that you may stumble on a really big idea. Talk to people your competitors wouldn't dream of talking to, and remember you are trying to do something different. Your coverage should be both multidisciplinary and multinational.

Unfortunately, in business life we meet and socialize with a narrow segment of people. These are usually colleagues at work, fellow members at the golf club, one's close family, and old school or college friends. How many of us are well known to a philosopher, a woman priest, a New Age traveler, a newspaper editor, a legislator, a judge, a law enforcer, an ex-prisoner or a psychologist? These are people who every day influence the pace of change in society. Their views are often the barometer of things to come, and yet how infrequently we come into contact with them.

Listen to Sue Shipman of the National Council for One-parent Families and you'll learn how the family structure has changed out of all recognition to what it was ten years ago. Observe the nerds in your local video café and you'll sense the obsession with the Internet. Talk to a newly ordained woman priest and you'll gain early insights into the ascent of women in society. Talk to an organizer for the American Association of Retired Persons and you'll get a feeling for how powerful and influential the ageing part of the US population is in influencing policy.

In identifying the forces of change, interview as many people as you can who have an impact on influencing the direction of change. Think as widely as you can outside the confines of your existing mind-set. Begin with your customer, then your customer's customer, and maybe the next one down the line. Think of all the factors and groups of people that may influence the customer chain.

Say you're a supplier of telephone switchgear. You should be talking to legislators to see how future policy may affect public procurement policy, potential entertainment and media providers, town planners, technologists with alternative solutions, economists to forecast alternative growth rates, social scientists who have thought about the structure of the family, and the home and human resource professionals who have views on the future of work and so on.

Poignancy

The more vivid the output the more poignant its meaning. Scenarios are not about estimating the number of buyers for a new product. They're about imagining what your customers might be like in the future. We shall be looking at various devices to enrich one's imagination.

In developing the scenarios in this book we used two devices which appeared to be successful in creating a vision for the customer of the future. The design and layout of news-stories for a newspaper of the future were intended to give an impression of what the typical headlines of the day might be in a particular scenario. "Two die in strike-ridden home" was meant to convey a number of themes. Firstly, a substantial number of jobs might be created in service industries looking after elderly people. Secondly, these would be poorly paid jobs and staff would be frequently urged to strike in order to demand more wages. Thirdly, they may be subject to a considerable degree of emotional blackmail as public pressure might force them to consider the effect of their strike action on the fate of their wards.

In my experience, there is a budding news editor in many of us, and the scenario-building teams I have worked with have enjoyed putting together the headlines and news-stories. Some with a fertile imagination can get quite carried away with their task and create some of the most vivid stories I have ever seen.

Another device which created realism with devastating effect was the development of a short play to depict the two-tier scenario. While presenting the scenario which consists of a world of "alrights" and "lo-eds" we staged an attempt by militant "lo-eds" to take a group of hostages at a meeting of a group of London executives. A Colombian manager of a multinational company told me that he had never been so frightened in his life by a piece of theatre. The text of the short play is given in the appendix on p. 225.

The Mid-Life Times *newspaper. An illustration of life in the future.*

The steps to scenario development

There are five steps to developing scenarios:

- Choose the area of investigation
- Establish the vectors of change
- Prepare the team
- Develop antithetical outcomes
- Identify scenarios via common themes

We discuss each step in turn.

Steps to developing scenarios

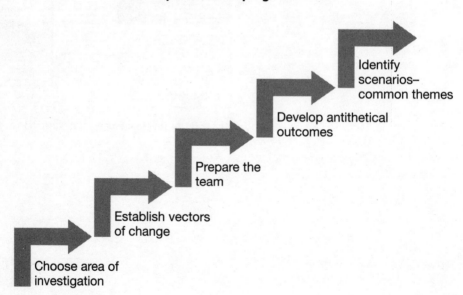

■ Choose the area of investigation

In developing scenarios for this book we stuck to a rather broad definition of the customer and considered the customer from a global point of view. The question "are we seeing the emergence of a global customer?" may be perfectly valid but more often you might want to know what, for instance, the South Asian consumer might be like 20 years from now or indeed what are the likely scenarios for consumer values in the travel industry worldwide. So we may have geographically specific scenarios or global scenarios for an industry segment. We may even want to get more specific and examine the possible future for a new product range such as zero-calorie chocolate in North America: a narrow product segment in a confined area of geography.

The narrower the area of investigation the deeper we can go into examining the future scenarios. You will constantly be caught between balancing the breadth and depth of the review. Some vectors will have greater relevance to your alternatives and some may only be vaguely connected. The wider your question the more vectors you will need to cover.

■ Establish the vectors of change

The vectors of change are the important factors which may affect the outcome of a particular scenario. It has been likened to someone steering a ship from a point A to a point B and having to encounter a number of different wind and current vectors. The experienced navigator steers the ship using the vectors to get from one point to another. We used the term vectors of change because a vector describes both speed and direction. We need to know in which direction a particular force of change is headed. If globalization is a force of change, then which way does it appear to be headed? Are governments accepting that their authority might be eroded by the power of international markets and business? Do citizens accept that their jobs and futures may be determined by some executive in Detroit or Seoul?

It has been likened to someone steering a ship from a point A to a point B.

Establish the vectors of change

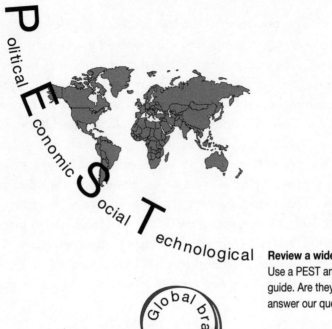

Review a wide range of vectors
Use a PEST analysis as an initial guide. Are they relevant, do they help answer our question?

RESEARCH relevant vectors deeply
Interviews, literature, key events

Identifying the vectors of change will depend on the area of investigation. The process should go something like this:

Review a wide spectrum of likely vectors

Part 2 should be a useful start to perform a quick scan of all the likely areas that might affect, say, your consumer of chocolate. Make a note of the potential areas and come back to them once you have read the entire section. These should form the backbone of your research. A useful check is the traditional PEST (political, economic, social, and technological) analysis, which tends to encompass most things which affect our lives.

Conduct a research program based on the identified vectors

Your research program should include interviews with both the most likely and the most unlikely people who might be influencers of one of your vectors.

So in addition to interviewing a dietician for the likely future in weight loss programs, you may also want to speak to fashion designers on the social image of overweightedness. Don't forget those who espouse purity in everything we eat and what impact an artificial product which masquerades as chocolate might have in a world where organic, traditional products are valued more than artificial ones. Conduct a thorough literature search on anything anyone has said or written about on the vectors which are relevant to you. You will begin to spot vectors in everything you read after a while. In researching the vectors for this book, I read all I could lay my hands on for months on end: newspapers from the gutter press to the quality publications like the *Wall Street Journal* and the *Financial Times*; vox pop magazines like *Hello* to high-brow worthy ones like *The Economist*; book reviews of the latest ghosted output from sports icons to the biographies of the intelligentsia; and film reviews of the latest releases from toon town to the serious world of documentary television. You will begin to take on the form of a walking encyclopedia of knowledge. Where necessary, commission others to carry out an investigation into areas where you neither have the time to investigate nor the detailed understanding of the issues. With the assembled forces you can now begin the process of building the scenarios.

■ Prepare the team

Your scenario-building team should be composed of the key members of your management team who need to collectively buy-in to the strategy being developed or the investments being made. You need these people for at least two days. That is, 48 hours, not two lots of eight hours. The exercise requires immersion in the future and in the vectors of change. It is difficult to get people caught up in the day-to-day operational chores of running a business and expect them to think about the future in one huge step. Usually the most creative breakthroughs come in the last few hours of a scenario workshop.

Ask people to come with an open mind and to suspend judgment on their colleagues during discussion time. Many of the ideas put out by participants may sound crazy at first, but it's usually the craziest of ideas that provide a fertile arena for innovation and product development.

In an exercise I once ran for a client in the brewing-to-pubs business, we began to develop a version of the "two-tier world" scenario where people would be too frightened to take the occasional walk to the pub. Specially-

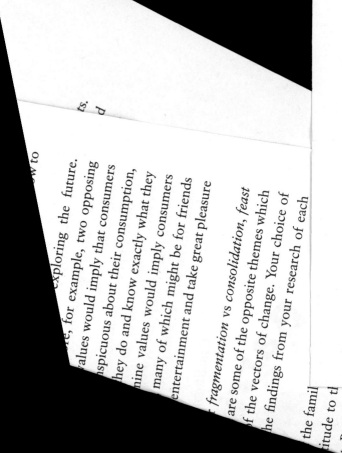

chauffeured limousines might collect prospective patrons and ferry them to a place where they might quench their thirst. "Why don't we do that now?" said one participant. Drinking and driving was already taboo and this ruled out a huge section of customers who might live more than a stagger away from the nearest pub. Whilst at the pub, patrons might actually feel free to take that extra drink, having passed on the responsibility of getting home to someone else. Thus the "limos for pubs" idea was born.

To begin a scenario workshop you need to get the group feeling free to think expansively about the future. I have found that a good loosening up exercise is to get the participants to carry out an exercise in envisioning on a topic which may be totally unconnected with the current problems of the day. One exercise taught to me by Henry Berry of Theory B, which always works, begins with asking participants to brainstorm the consequences of "imagine that all desks have been found to be redundant. Find as many uses as you can for them." The group then proceeds to find as many uses as it can for the redundant desks. Mildly interesting ideas such as converting them into hospital beds begin the exercise, with the ideas getting wilder until the desks are being sawn in half to be used as magicians' tables or as contraceptive devices for large elephants. The group now has permission to be outrageous.

Entering the circle of change

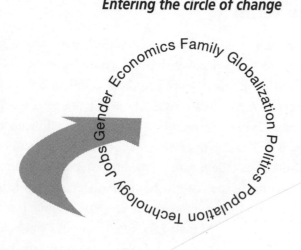

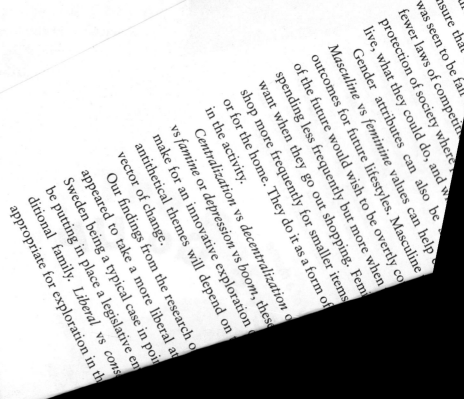

The two opposite outcomes

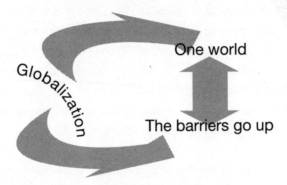

■ Developing antithetical outcomes

The next step is to introduce the vectors of change in turn to the participants. The research conducted for each vector needs to be presented and discussed fully to air additional points which each participant may feel adds to or supplements the research. The group then debates two opposite consequences of that vector. We refer to this as entering the circle of change, as we shall see later how many of the outcomes of each vector have common themes which we shall call scenarios.

Say the two opposite consequences of "Globalization" are: *One world (the continuous breaking down of barriers)* and *The barriers go up (backlash)*. One half of the group debates the consequences of the former and the other half discusses the latter. They both present their deliberations to each other.

Constituents of a theme

- Ingredients e.g. capital, technology, laws
- Results e.g. world trade declines
- Product/services e.g. local brands

We find that antithetical outcomes are a good way of getting people to think through the consequences of each driving force. *Liberalism* vs *conservatism*, for example, would create a number of different outcomes for where the institution of the family might be headed. A liberal set of values would support young single mothers, and after some time we might find that the total structure of the family has changed and that society gets more accepting of one-parent families. A conservative stance would suggest that society tries to resist the change in family values and imposes constraints on married couples that wish to separate.

Individualism vs *collectivism* is a good way to consider the politics of the future. An individualistic outcome would warrant stringent state laws to ensure that individuals do not violate the rights of others, that competition was seen to be fair via anti-monopoly laws. A collectivist outcome would have fewer laws of competition, as business believes in self-regulation, and more of protection of society where people would expect the state to tell them how to live, what they could do, and what was forbidden.

Gender attributes can also be a useful way of exploring the future. *Masculine* vs *feminine* values can help explore, for example, two opposing outcomes for future lifestyles. Masculine values would imply that consumers of the future would wish to be overtly conspicuous about their consumption, spending less frequently but more when they do and know exactly what they want when they go out shopping. Feminine values would imply consumers shop more frequently for smaller items, many of which might be for friends or for the home. They do it as a form of entertainment and take great pleasure in the activity.

Centralization vs *decentralization* or *fragmentation* vs *consolidation, feast* vs *famine* or *depression* vs *boom,* these are some of the opposite themes which make for an innovative exploration of the vectors of change. Your choice of antithetical themes will depend on the findings from your research of each vector of change.

Our findings from the research of the family indicated that some countries appeared to take a more liberal attitude to the changes in family structure, Sweden being a typical case in point. Both Singapore and Britain appeared to be putting in place a legislative environment to reverse the decline in the traditional family. *Liberal* vs *conservative* contrary themes appeared to be appropriate for exploration in this case.

Typical antithetical outcomes

Fragmentation	⟷	Consolidation
Liberalism	⟷	Conservatism
Individualism	⟷	Collectivism
Decentralization	⟷	Centralization
Masculine	⟷	Feminine

■ Presenting the antithetical outcomes

Let us see how each antithetical outcome can be presented by an example of the output presented by the two groups looking at the consequences of globalization.

A. The barriers go up (backlash)

A backlash is created by the continual drift away of jobs from the developed world. The emerging world is convinced that multinationals are taking them for a ride and decide to nationalize and throw the "foreigners" out. There would be a substantial change in the post-war world order. These are the key ingredients:

- *Capital* – nationalistic institutions would impede investment flows.
- *Labor* – unions, supported by the state, would put up barriers to prevent the export of jobs.
- *Goods* – governments would introduce a variety of legislation to stop the importation of goods through anti-dumping and unfair competition laws.
- *Information* – nations would resist the free flow of communication to stop its citizens from wanting the lifestyles of other better-off countries. They would conspire to jam satellite television and pull the plug on the Net.

The results

Trade blocs would develop to lock out unwelcome competition. Fortress Europe would annex Eastern Europe as a back door for cheap manufacturing and agriculture. Tariffs would rise, leading to prices going up and efficiency down. This might present short-term benefits for both US and Europe by arresting the slide in unemployment and protecting welfare. But in the longer term the lack of export growth would lead to stagnation.

Much tougher immigration policies would be enacted to further bolster the fortress mentality, with more of an emphasis on skill-based immigration. German influence would dominate Europe without the counter-balancing influence of Japan and America. Several long-standing international treaties would be broken and trade deals would have to be negotiated bloc-to-bloc. Russia would become Europe's raw material supplier and Nato's role would become redundant.

The role of the nation state would be emphasized via federal alliances of countries, and bureaucrats would become all-powerful: Eurocrats and US State Department comptrollers would be as powerful as leaders of state. The bureaucrats would establish elaborate defense mechanisms against external threats and would have primacy in meeting demands for special interest areas to protect local jobs. The biggest internal threat to the developed world would be adapting to nil or negative population growth.

In every fortress-like trading bloc each country would begin to become more and more suspicious of the other in terms of getting a fair deal out of a diminishing amount of economic means. Nationalism would rear its head and other attendant phenomena such as racism, fascism, and tribalism would begin to plague any federation.

Products/services

Products would need extensive national customization, and even within trading blocs, seeking economies of scale from a single large market for products and services would be difficult. Branding would be strictly on the basis of regional or national tastes, and the consumer's choice of competing global brands would begin to become heavily restricted.

Global air fares would rise because of protection of air routes and because people would not travel as extensively. Communication would be restricted to specially legislated areas where people's diet of the media would be controlled in terms of what the bureaucrats felt was desirable to avoid mass disaffection of the population. Common languages such as English would diminish in importance and there would be a proliferation of national languages, and many extinct languages would be revived.

In the developing world, industrialization would slow and might even be halted. The disaffected youth in an African or South American theater might be wooed by a Maoist-type figure and bring a period of great instability to global politics.

The newly industrialized world of South-East Asia would initially attempt to satisfy its regional demand growth and would be successful in doing this for a while. Prosperity would last for not more than a decade, after which lack of global trading and technology exchange would cause these regions to stagnate and begin a period of decline. An arms race might provide temporary respite for its defense industries.

B. One world (the continuous breaking down of barriers)

Barriers to world trade begin to tumble as nations begin to believe that world trade is conducive to long-term growth. China needs food, raw materials, and technology to fuel its enormous expansion. India needs access to lucrative software contracts in the West. The West needs markets for its branded consumer products. These are the key ingredients:

- *Politics* – the realization that centralized command economies do not work.
- *Scale* – companies seek economies of scale by global branding.
- *Communications* – satellite television does more to create global awareness than any other medium before it.
- *Networks* – cheap networking technology such as the Internet promotes business in cyberspace, completely independent of geography.
- *Americana* – younger generations are lured to the appeal of American culture as depicted in advertising, pop culture, and films.

The results

Huge economies of scale would result in a potential doubling of global customers in 20 years. Branded products like Coca-Cola would witness unprecedented growth, and manufacturers of technology products such as computer chips would be able to step up their investment in research and development. Technology will become affordable to more people and its shelf-life will continue to shorten.

The old developed world will concentrate on industries which involve the information-intensive service sectors such as insurance, banking, and trading. Development of consumer products for the mature markets of the West will be used as the leading edge of global product strategies. The building of vast media factories which provide content for the proliferating channels of communication will employ significant numbers of people.

Design and development will be decoupled from construction and production. Thus a technology company may conduct all its research and development in Palo Alto and contract construction of software, for example, to a factory in Bangalore and assembly of hardware components to another facility on the west coast of Ireland. The process is not unlike a pharmaceutical company undertaking R&D for a new cure.

Variety will flourish together with convergence in global values. Sports, business, and music might take on a global convergence of tastes and practices, yet rites and rituals and symbols which give people a sense of belonging and identity, will become important. An Arab businessman might wear a suit to a business meeting but wear traditional Arab garments to a social occasion. Young Indian adults might attend all-night raves, yet adhere to arranged marriages. Londoners might be cosmopolitan in their eating habits all year yet stick to turkey for Christmas every year.

Customs and trade barriers will have ceased to exist in all but minimal form and global electronic trading would have accelerated the end of these barriers. The countries which maintain high taxes will witness a migration of the most skilled and employable individuals to areas of low taxation and open borders. The global worker can live anywhere, and rudimentary English will become a language of common communication with three billion people who will have learnt it as a second language.

The world's big global cities will be occupied by locals (those who live and work locally) and cosmopolitans (those who live and work globally). Cosmopolitans will drift seamlessly between countries of the world, usually engaged by some major corporation. Locals will support the service industries which grow up to support global corporations.

Environmental impact will be planned globally by a fusion of business and intergovernmental organizations, and trade-offs will be made with developing countries that cannot afford the high clean-up costs. A consortium of European countries will jointly fund the $4 billion decommissioning program for Chernobyl to protect the whole of Western Europe from the likely fall-out of a reactor failure.

Products and services

Products which slow or reverse the ageing process will be the new global consumer market, and consumers will pay considerable sums of money to "keep young" in this high-margin business. Health concerns will change living and eating habits, and sports personalities will be used to endorse healthy products globally.

A certain universality of youth will pervade the world where teenagers and young adults will buy the same branded clothes, listen to the same music, eat the same fast food, and consume the same drinks. Upscale brands which are outward manifestations of wealth will be more popular in the emerging economies, where "conspicuous" consumption will be valued. In mature markets consumers will continue to yearn for luxury products but prefer to be more private about their wealth. "Old money" will compete with "new money."

Countries will attempt to export their culture, and those with strongly differentiated images will succeed enormously. France will export the quality of its cuisine through consumer food companies, Ireland's friendly pub will be branded globally by Guinness, entertainment companies will exploit North America's youth culture, and Japanese design will be exploited in automobiles.

Education will be globalized top down. The leading business schools will offer distance learning down the Net and bring MBAs within the affordability of many the world over. Later, other specialized tertiary educational qualifications in economics, media, and design or international finance may be offered by both private and state institutions. Finally, expect policing of international standards of both primary and secondary education to ensure educational qualifications are valid globally.

The protection of trademarks will stamp out piracy in most parts of the world, and companies will be able to simultaneously release copyright material globally without fear of losing revenue. This will keep international patent registration agencies busy. Brand names which wish to trade in certain parts of the world will have to buy out sound-alike firms who could claim they were there first.

Identifying scenarios from common themes

The fewer the scenarios one has to contend with the better. I have found that three is the maximum most people can visualize at any one time, and two scenarios offer the greatest simplicity. You should therefore always try, where possible, to develop two or three themes to the outcomes generated.

When we generated outcomes for the customer of the future we found that every time we entered the circle of change we would emerge with certain underlying connections. The mid-life crisis scenario was borne out of the associations we made in one set of outcomes with the recurring theme of conservatism and resistance to radical change, the greying of politics and the disillusionment with politicians, the rise in feminine values, the protection of the family institution, post-consumer values, the concern for the environment, and the effects of a gradual ageing of populations in the developed world.

The two-tier world was made up of a series of linkages with a growing fear of globalization, the putting up of barriers, the rise of tribalism, the pursuit of individualism (I'm alright), the breakdown of the family, a backlash against women, education for the very privileged, and the growing rift between rich and poor.

Drawing these linkages can be quite easy when the group has begun to develop a few outcomes. It often helps to pause for a few hours or even overnight to "see the picture." At a retreat in Wales, where I have held most of my scenario planning sessions, we have gone for a walk by the Pembrokeshire Coastal Path to allow the sea breezes to breathe life into our thinking.

Peter Schwartz talks of a scenario being like a story. I extended this idea to a film. Most people have their favorite films and their worst, and films are an excellent mechanism for capturing a theme, a time, or a place. Films too are becoming a fairly universal idiom and lend themselves to an international group. Recalling great books can also have the same effect.

"What film does this collection of ideas remind you of?" is a good way to get people thinking about their scenario. Peter Sellers' *I'm alright Jack* inspired the two-tier scenario for this book, and *Passages* by Gail Sheehy based on Jung's teaching gave birth to the mid-life crisis scenario.

■ Applying the scenarios

Once we have developed the scenarios we can set about using them in our business. We shall discuss below some of the uses we can put them to.

Testing your strategy

Scenarios are a good way to test your existing strategy or an intended one, to see how the enterprise might fare in the future. We are not trying to promote a particular path for the future but merely to test the robustness of the company to future vectors of change. How successful or how vulnerable will our company be if either of the scenarios were to predominate?

Taking the two scenarios described earlier in this book, it would appear that a customer proposition which focusses on value would succeed in either outcome. Mid-lifers are not conspicuous consumers and make purchases judiciously, using past experiences and referrals from friends and colleagues. Clothing must be known for its durability, food for its nutritional value, and cars for their trade-in value and low running costs.

In the two-tier world the vast majority of the consuming underclass would also make purchases based on value, with most transactions being price led. Assuming we cannot reverse the expectations of consumers on the quality of products, then the same proposition would hold true.

Old-established brands will also feature well under both scenarios provided they continue to invest in maintaining brand values. Mid-lifers remember the products they consumed when they were younger and frequently go back to them. Coca-Cola is drunk just as much by babyboomers as by teenagers. Coca-Cola also has the highest consumption in Mexico's two-tier society.

In 1995 ABB, the engineering company, British Airways, and Nestlé won an award for Europe's most admired companies. I reviewed their apparent existing strategies for the *Financial Times* and assessed their fate in 2015 according to the mid-life and two-tier scenarios.

The mid-life crisis scenario results in a big comeback for investment in railways. Older populations become more environmentally conscious and will have had enough of gridlock, car emissions causing asthma and other ailments, and will put pressure on governments to increase expenditure on clean public transport. In the post-modern world federations will prosper in favor of the nation state. The EU will become more integrated in its communications, transport, and by implication, railway systems.

ABB and its venture with Daimler-Benz makes it a clear leader in this $60 billion market. Helped by privatization of national railways and a subsequent move to standardization across countries, this market could grow at up to 8 percent per annum.

What is ABB's gain could be BA's challenge. The further integration of European railways could be a substantial threat to BA's short-haul flights. Operating margins on scheduled passengers has been falling and BA needs more short-haul passengers to improve margins. Railways take business travelers from city center to city center avoiding the delays of airport handling and transit to them. No doubt BA will need to apply innovative packaging of its future customers' door-to-door travel needs. Could we, for example, see a return of the airline luxury coach service with on-board check-in and security.

Environmental concerns will also resist further expansion of nuclear power in the West, and although ABB is active in the building of nuclear plants, its lead role in the decommissioning of the Chernobyl nuclear power reactor and the replacement with gas turbines positions it well, not only with the environmental groups but with the high likelihood of similar projects at other nuclear power plants in Europe. The state of other Eastern and Central European reactors such as those in Bulgaria are a cause for concern, and which over the next decade will undoubtedly need decommissioning and replacing in order to avoid another Chernobyl.

All scenarios assume expansion in Asian markets albeit in varying amounts and in different ways. For example, in the two-tier scenario Asia's consumer goods expansion is concentrated in a few upper and upper middle income consumers.

Asia is both a threat and an opportunity. Within the next decade it will account for the world's largest middle class market of brand-conscious consumers, eager to match or even exceed the living aspirations of their European counterparts. The ability of Europe's companies in competing for and winning market share from their US and Asian competitors will be not only a challenge but a necessity. Asia represents probably the biggest opportunity to enhance revenue and thereby increase shareholder value.

ABB has astounded us with the sensitivity with which it has changed its business into a truly global enterprise, both culturally and operationally. When faced with a cancellation of a $2.8 billion power plant in India, its CEO, Barnevik, in his sympathetic and understanding tone, commented, "We have no illusions. Things take longer there ... there are political twists and turns."

Contrast that with other corporate executives who faced with a similar dis-appointment would resort to aggressive talk of "never doing business with that lot again." ABB, that plans to invest $1 billion in India and produce a net income of $3 billion by the turn of the century, is in for the long-haul.

ABB's power generation business has organized into a global business seg-ment and has has been gearing up for a rapid increase in Asian business volume which it anticipates may actually triple. It has worked hard at cutting costs by sourcing from lower-cost countries in Central Europe and Asia. The proportion of equipment made in Europe and the US is down to about 50 percent.

The airline industry in the US may now have reached the peak of its business cycle. Future growth for BA may therefore only be possible in the expanding markets of Asia, where air traffic is expected to grow at above-average rates of 8 percent per year. Its agreement with Qantas could give it, in the long term, more of a strategic advantage than its tie-up with US-Air. BA are already talk-ing about extending the language capability of their cabin crew on the assump-tion that within the next decade there would be more passengers speaking Asian languages than English.

Nestlé's late but necessary entry into the Asian ice cream market will chal-lenge Unilever, the leader, and increase competition. However, double digit growth in this market should allow enough space for a few key players. Nestlé's strong brands in chocolates, confectionery, and beverages (Perrier, Nescafé) will do well with these new brand-conscious consumers. Nestlé's production facilities are spread around the world, many of them in low-cost, weak-cur-rency countries. This should allow the company to compete favorably in situ-ations where price will be a differentiator.

It gets increasingly difficult to market to consumers in the established mar-kets of the developed world. The proliferation of television channels and the variety of communication media, from the Internet to community-based newspapers and direct mail, will make traditional marketing ineffective. Customer interactions will be complex and over a wide range of channels. Only those companies that invest in understanding their customers well and manage those relationships successfully will succeed.

British Airways has already made considerable headway in customer rela-tionship management. Its frequent flyer club programs and customer service initiatives are well in keeping with any other in the industry. Nestlé on the other hand is handicapped by the increasing stranglehold retailers have on their suppliers, and the proliferation of own-label and price competition will make

*it difficult for consumer product companies to build loyalty with their cus-
tomers in traditional ways. Innovation in new products such as "flexible
chocolate", zero calorie candy and new distribution channels will be important if Nestlé is to grow in its established markets.*

*The rise of communitarianism will cause environmental and other socio-
political groups to have an increasing impact on company strategy, their
approach to the environment, and the transparency of their business ethics.
Companies will have to, in many cases, work with the most influential of these
groups rather than against them.*

*Nestlé's exposure in the infant nutrition and milk substitutes market could
cause it increasing problems in the mid-life scenario. Virtual communities such
as Cambridge-based Baby Milk Action could marshal their opposition more
cohesively on the Internet across the world bringing pressure on the company
to deemphasize this business. Conversely, in the two-tier scenario the same
business could boom.*

As an innovation engine

My own greatest success with scenario planning, and indeed the most reward-
ing, has been its use as an engine for innovation. Irrespective of whether any
particular scenario comes to pass, the key to a firm's success is often in shaping its own destiny. Working with some of the vectors of change, a company
can shape not only its own future but influence the structure of its own
market.

If women's earning power is increasing and more women are likely to be in
professional roles, then are their needs being fully met by a male-dominated
service industry? Would all-female hotels, pubs, and clubs be something for
the future and why shouldn't we be thinking about it today?

If welfare is going to fall more into private sector hands then what are we
doing to educate the underprovided-for pensioners of tomorrow so that they
need to be saving now for a more secure future? How do we introduce new
products to ensure that our pension funds will return investors a source of
income well into their advanced years.

If I'm a provider of mortgage finance, how do I convince potential mort-
gagees that the variability in their future personal income, because of flexible
working patterns, can be accommodated? Are there specific financing
schemes for the portfolio worker of tomorrow that we need to be thinking
about today?

If institutional investors, my customers of capital, are going to be increasing in their power and influence then how do I as CEO of a major corporation manage the expectations of this group? Should I be thinking now about a more inclusive form of governance for the company, which provides access and accountability to these groups without compromising my competitive position?

Does the prospect of global warming and environmental concerns turn "green" issues from a minority to a majority concern? As a major publisher of newspapers should I be thinking about the idea of the recyclable newspaper: give us back your old papers and we'll give you our new edition in return? As a retailer of wines or bottled beverages, would an incentive to return bottles belonging to the company not only help to increase customer retention but also satisfy consumers' environmental concerns regarding the quantity of waste which we dispose of every day?

Given the growing concerns for security and rising crime would my company, the provider of security systems, do well to consider offering a bundled service including the insurance of your property: buy our systems and we'll offer you the best insurance deal around?

Innovation engine workshops generate dozens of opportunities and they are all orientated towards future revenue-generating ideas. Quite some way from Gary Hamel's concern about corporate anorexia.

Professor Kees Van der Heijden refers to this type of research as customer "concept engineering." We need to try to understand the various influences on the customer and develop a vision for what the customer needs might be in the future. Something which traditional market research and focus group techniques do not give us.

In 1995 AT&T decoupled its computer business which it acquired as NCR half a decade earlier. Was this a lost opportunity for AT&T? Doing business internationally consumes vast time and effort, traveling to meetings around the world. We saw earlier in one of our scenarios that in the future, international executives will conduct most meetings with colleagues around the world sat at their desk rather than spending 300 days a year on planes. Is this something AT&T should have been taking a lead on by coupling to their networks a cheap desk-top device developed by their computer division and creatively packaging a cut-travel-and-improve-your-family-life type of service?

Alas, AT&T as a carrier is a commodity service without much differentiation. Companies like AT&T caught up in tough price-based competition need to think about customer concepts before they become mainstream and have products in place to shape the market at the right time.

Innovation workshops should consider both innovation in the product and in the service delivered to customers. Which features incorporated in the product would deliver real customer value and perhaps which features inhibit value. A good example of this is gadgetry in home electronics. For much of the 1980s we appeared to have an insatiable thirst for electronic add-ons in Hi-Fi, VCRs and cameras. Features were used to sell equipment: the more the better. Integrated chips made the incremental cost of these features negligible. Today, we've grown up with electronics and we want simplicity with lots of quality. One control does it all on some of the most expensive Hi-Fis. One or two of the quality brands had spotted this trend some time ago and begun to sell simplicity ahead of their competitors who were still making cameras look like Christmas trees and VCRs like a NASA controller's panel.

In an innovation workshop I conducted for my own firm we looked at the opportunities for differentiating our core product, the audit. Auditing has been becoming more of a commodity with the increased use of information systems and fewer large complex companies to audit. Our look at the vectors affecting the business showed that the privatization of welfare would increase investment in equities via pension funds and large managed investment plans. Fund managers were becoming powerful interventionists in the management of the companies they invested in. The audit of the future needed to accommodate the needs of these new stakeholders, who were most interested in the future performance of their stock, rather than an historical look back at the company's past year of trading. The audit therefore needed to be more forward looking than it had traditionally been.

The service proposition too is an area where innovation can be used to get ahead of the competition. Customer value is derived from the point of sale, through use and at the point of disposal or abandonment of the product. Innovation in the service proposition comes from looking at the points in the product life cycle where customers may derive value in the future. Grocery retailers need to consider the changing nature of the family and the lack of available time for single working people to shop for food. Automobile distributors need to be aware of the trend from "ownership" to "custodianship;" away from outright purchases of cars towards renting or buying. The life insurance company needs to be aware of the changing employment patterns of its customers and their variable set of circumstances and ability to afford regular premiums. Scenarios are a rich source of ideas to help you plug future gaps in the service proposition.

Take as an example some of the hottest air routes in Europe, between London and Paris, Brussels or Amsterdam. If you were based in London the English Channel has up until recently ensured that to do a day's business in Paris you would have to take a plane. That would mean driving or using the transportation system to get to London's Heathrow airport, checking in, queuing for security inspections and finally boarding the aircraft. You would have to go through the same procedures the other end in Paris.

Then someone builds a tunnel between the two countries and you can take a train from city centre to city centre in three hours, sitting in a comfortable chair as though you were in your office. How do you respond if you were one of the airlines and a major portion of your revenue was about to disappear?

You might look at one or two scenarios and see if they provide the answer. If the business traveler is your prime target then you will need to explore the vectors of work and how they might affect your future customers.

One theme might be *The World Cities* scenario where cities like London and Paris become magnets for international companies who wish to base their operations there. Through these key centers the world's corporations would conduct their trade and attract large numbers of smaller service companies who would also wish to be based close to their clients. In Ross Moss-Kanter's terms, these world cities would be made up of *locals* and *cosmopolitans*. The latter would travel extensively. Cosmopolitans would always be a short taxi or limousine drive away from a railway station.

The other theme might be *The Satellite* scenario where companies move out of decaying, congested cities and set up their operations in less crowded towns and industrial complexes several miles away from London and Paris. Although they maintain small satellite offices in the city, these are nominal facilities usually for the Chairman to meet visiting VIPs. Most of the management may telecommute from offices in their homes in leafy suburbs using advanced telecommunication facilities. The city center railway station may be further away than the airport and might be difficult to get to, particularly during the rush hours.

The airline could be complacent and hope that the second scenario might prevail. If it did it would be putting itself at some considerable risk of potential market share erosion. One factor common to both scenarios is that the executive of the future will have to be increasingly judicious with his or her time, needing to grab every available minute of the day to keep on top of events within the company and externally with customers, shareholders and suppliers. Anything the airline can do to help make more time available for productive work would be seen to be adding enormous customer value.

A pick-up service to the airport, automatic check-in by the driver of your vehicle and direct boarding on to the plane, completely eliminating the time spent in lounges and waiting areas, would reduce by more than half the amount of wasted time. In monetary terms this may be equivalent to between $100 to $500 of an executive's time. A pick-up service would also insulate the airline against the World City scenario because by turning up at the customer's departure point, the airline is taking total responsibility for a door-to-door service. This would then seem a piece of innovation which is valid for both scenarios.

■ Scenario milestones

As you progress towards a point in the future in which your scenarios are based, you will wish to know which one is dominant. It is unlikely that we will live in a world which is the exclusive preserve of one scenario. As we progress into the future, certain key events or critical measures should provide clues as to where our market might be headed.

Key events might be the end of a term of office for a statesman or indeed his death. Most China watchers have the death of Deng prominent on their radar screens as a key event, the aftermath of which will determine the possible fate of South-East Asia next century. The handover of Hong Kong after 1997 is another key event connected with the future fate of South-East Asia. If the PRC allows the British colony to continue running its economy unimpeded then the world will be assured of Asia's growth and dominance as an economic powerhouse.

Other key events might be the signing of treaties or trade pacts. The formation of a single European currency would be a key event to track. Further new agreement on GATT, the extension of the PRC's most favored nation status and some potential breakthrough on open skies for the world's airlines would be other examples of key events.

Tracking the future

Key events

Vectoral measures

Magadisaster Scientific breakthrough Election Trade agreement Market collapse Deng's death

Savings rates Air travel Opinion research Employment trends Income differences

N
W——E
S

Key vectoral measures can be another useful means to track the future. The number of women gaining jobs or professional qualifications would point to a future of more women in higher management ranks. This would create a new group of customers with emerging unfulfilled needs. Several regular employment surveys are available to help track employment patterns.

The percentage of people in part-time vs full-time work will tell you if work patterns are getting more variable. The growth in small businesses is also a key vectoral measure to help track the move towards self-employment and port-folio working.

Wage differences will tell you if the gap between lo-eds and alrights is increasing, and indeed the percentage of the unemployed and those below the poverty line. On a world scale, a worsening of the indebtedness of the poor countries and the risk factors associated with countries give you a measure of an increasing likelihood of the two-tier scenario on a world scale.

Opinion research is also a powerful way to capture the direction of a par-ticular scenario. Watch for liberal attitudes to sex, divorce, drugs, and minori-ties. Equally, look for signs of a reaction to all these issues. A two-tier world evokes gut instincts in human beings who are struggling to meet their basic living needs. The starving hunter cannot afford to be magnanimous about the hare he has just caught.

■ Consulting the oracle – using sample scenarios to make decisions

Here are some examples of how you can use future scenarios to make decisions which may be critical to the success of your organization and in one concluding example, to yourself.

What will be the future of books?

As a publisher of fiction and non-fiction you may wish to plan your future investment strategy. How could scenarios help you to position your own product strategy?

The mid-life scenario offers us a world where the word goes digital. People get used to taking their information as sound bytes. Shakespeare in 15 minutes, War and Peace in 20 minutes with the sound of battle and the music of Tchaikovsky thrown in for good measure. A new literature is born, "Digiture." Books go digital combining all the advantages of multimedia and reinventing the medium which Gutenberg created 400 years ago. Books in their traditional format will not disappear. People will cherish books as an expression of traditional values, the older generation boomers of the 60s will seek out books which are thought pieces in 20th century literature. Expect fewer reference books, most of them being digitized, but we can still look forward to a steady stream of fiction and the thinking person's book; something you can take to bed, sit in the bath with, or get stuck into on a beach.

In the two-tier scenario literacy levels have fallen dramatically. Only the alrights can read. Alrights buy books for prestige value, usually leather bound and a great outward manifestation of esteem and position. Reading a book can be symbolic of being part of the Alright set. Books adorn private shelves and are purchased by the well-off by the metre for their appearance, rather than their content. The lo-eds in contrast do not read and don't buy books; most of their reading comes from simple broadsheets which assume a vocabulary of not more than a thousand words. Speech is the main form of communication. Periodically *lo-eds may burn books and pillage book shops as a sign of their frustration and anger with not being able to share the same privileges as alrights.*

In either scenario, books will survive, albeit customers will regard them in a different light; something of great personal value in one scenario or something of status in the other. In both scenarios we may assume that books will not be the main medium for conveying words and ideas. The reference book for example may all but disappear with the advent of "digiture" or become a minority requirement in the two-tier scenario. The traditional novel on the other hand will have a long-term future.

Homes of the future

Imagine I'm in the building business, constructing homes for people to live in. Times are getting bad, there are fewer government backed "home starts" and with the growing insecurity of people's jobs they do not want to commit to long term mortgages. I need to bring some focus to my activities in order to survive. What should I do?

Let's take the vector which corresponds to demographics and population growth; one of the basic drivers of accommodation needs. The ageing population is a given fact which is not open to debate and no matter which scenario we look at, we cannot escape the fact that our Western societies are getting older. Assume that as people begin to age their need for large houses recede and once their children have left home they want to live in smaller premises which are easier to run and maintain. These homes should ideally have some social centre because the older you get the less mobile you are and the more you need other people at hand to fall back on in times of illness.

Another vector of some significance might be the privatization of welfare. The state may be less able to provide for the housing needs of its citizens and people may have to take on more responsibility for the provision of their basic needs such as accommodation, education and so on. The shift of responsibility therefore from the state to the individual will create a number of opportunities for the private sector.

Now let's look at the antithetical outcomes over which we have little influence. They derive from the "family" vector and produce radically different scenarios but surprisingly similar responses. The "*micro family*" and the "*extended family*" are at two opposite ends of the spectrum.

In the micro family we see changes continuing with single parent units and loosely coupled cohabiting partners, together with more people living on their own. Marriage as an institution for permanent life-long relationships is replaced by a type of serial monogamy where couples get together for a number of years and then go their separate ways. The mother becomes the basis for continuity of the family. "Solitaires," the single unattached people, spend most of their time at work or out socializing with office colleagues and the home for them may be a place to sleep and find a clean set of clothes. In other words their accommodation needs are minimal.

In the extended family scenario, society acts to reverse the trend in the breakup of the nuclear family by the use of tax and legislative incentives. Children who leave home, only do so temporarily, finding that they cannot afford the cost of living away. Many even marry and live with their parents. The extended unit finds that the bigger the family, the better its overall standard of living; grandparents look after children while the parents go to work, the grandparents in turn are less isolated, the children feel more secure with familiar surroundings. In other words we may be reverting to the family model that existed before the industrial revolution and which still exists today in many Eastern cultures.

There are some common themes to these scenarios. Families will require variability in their accommodation needs; while raising children they may need a three-bed-roomed house, later a single bed apartment might suffice. They will also crave the need for security of a roof over their heads. Thirdly they will want to keep at least the same standard of accommodation they have enjoyed throughout their working lives.

The "house for life" may actually capture most of the requirements of all three scenarios. You contract with your customers to provide them with tradeable units of housing which they own for the rest of their lives. As their circumstances change they have the option of either trading up to gain more units or down to pass units on to their children. Trading up can either gain them more accommodation or relocate them to a higher cost area. The actual standard of the homes does not vary. You can buy units on the same estate or split your units between two estates. You can insure your customers for loss of earnings due to unforeseen circumstances and you can carry out customizations such as painting, decoration, special fixtures and fittings which are removable but provide that much needed touch of individuality. The housing design is clustered to create a community, which is attractive to both the aged and young families. Your building company will need to rebrand itself from a "constructor of houses" to an organization which accommodates the trend to the privatization of welfare; an organization which "provides for your lifelong accommodation needs." Your future employees would not only be engineers, architects, and tradesmen but also social scientists and care workers and you would almost certainly want to enter into an alliance with a financial institution to provide the various add-on services of finance and insurance.

Personal scenario development

Question: Is my career better served
outside this organization?

Consolidated

Work/
organization

Specialism

Fragmented

Specialization of skills

Change vectors & antithetical themes

Outsourced skills

Decision: Leave now

Personal scenario planning

Working on future scenarios has led me inevitably to think about where I fit into this future world. What the next 20 years might mean for my ambitions, my career and my children. What skills should I be acquiring, what subjects should my sons major in at university, where should I be investing for the future? These are questions which will undoubtedly have gone through your mind while reading this book.

Scenarios are an effective way of beginning to think through the issues and making an informed decision. The process is similar to the one we looked at earlier in this chapter. Begin by deciding which question you want to answer and then look at the vectors of change which are likely to affect your decision before developing antithetical outcomes and eventually the scenarios.

Let's say you want to make a decision whether to leave full-time employment and become a self-employed consultant or stay on and take your chances up the corporate ladder.

One of the vectors of change which would be most relevant to your decision would probably be the future of work. You would research the future of work in the proximity of your skills area by reading about experts' views and interviewing people who may be in the industry you operate in. You may also wish to seek the views of existing and potential customers.

Say you are an economist. Your research may indicate that work patterns for economists are changing and that companies are outsourcing the skills that you have developed. Currently companies buy-in the services of economists both from one-man consultants and the larger firms. The market is a fragmented one.

The two antithetical outcomes for work in your industry are: economists' services become more fragmented with greater specialization and many more niches created, or the market consolidates because of variable quality and reliability and big firms wipe out the one-man consultancies. In one outcome you would thrive, in the other you would starve unless you were able to join one of the big firms; not always easy unless you bring along a healthy client portfolio.

Another vector which may affect your decision is the shrinking world. If business is increasingly conducted in cyberspace, you will be able to offer specialist skills to a world market. No longer will you be confined to your local market. On the other hand if technology bombs and all the promises of the vast expansion in the Internet fizzle out you're on your own. Throw in slow growth rates in your home markets and you're in for a tough time.

You can see two scenarios beginning to emerge: a fragmented consulting industry in which you would prosper and a consolidating industry in which you might be squeezed out. Your only way of ensuring that you have a long term future would be to ensure you develop a strong client portfolio, which might only be possible by specialization in a particular industry.

Meanwhile what's life like in your own company?

In the fragmented scenario, the company has to fight hard to maintain or grow market share whilst in a consolidating scenario your company is acquired or merged with another company. In both scenarios, the future of the organization you work for looks increasingly bleak. Your decision to stay would perhaps be unwise. The company may be currently offering a generous severance package. Take it and leave.

Shareholder value – The top ten

And finally if this book has not added any value so far, you might wish to consider using the vectors of change described earlier to organize your own investment portfolio for the future. The vectors of change point to certain sectors where companies should do particularly well in terms of adding long term shareholder value. Here is a list of the top ten performers over the next decade.

1 Fund management and pensions

Companies offering personal fund management services will do particularly well with the privatization of welfare and the steadily ageing population being the major drivers. Personal pensions, healthcare, job protection and care for the aged will create increasing market demand throughout the Western world. Savings rates will steadily increase and higher income earners will look to the capital markets to preserve their income in the long term.

2 Food

The combination of adding 2 billion people to this planet over the next 20 years and the rising economic prosperity of countries like China will put great demands on the production and distribution of food throughout the world. All companies involved in the supply of food to global markets could be good investments for shareholders.

3 Software

The demand for software will be insatiable. Driven by the escalating power of computing and by the increase in networked communications over the next five years we could see up to an additional half a billion users of networked software by the turn of the century. An early agreement on software piracy could further fill the coffers of software providers.

4 Water

The sourcing, distribution and recycling of water over the next 20 years will attract much investor attention as acquifers, springs and other sources of water dry up. Climate changes will deplete supply in currently populated areas and water will rise from its existing super-commodity status to a higher valued resource. Water companies will be sought after by other acquisitive companies and will themselves seek to consolidate their distribution activities with others in the industry.

5 Security

The increasing gap between the high and low income earners will increase worries of personal security and all companies in the provision of assuring personal safety and protection of assets will see rising demand. Surveillance equipment providers, bodyguards, and private policing services should perform well, provided these organizations carefully regulate their recruitment practices.

6 Transport

The shrinking world gives rise to an increase in air transport with up to 200 million additional visitors being added to long haul routes around the world.

The train supplants short haul routes in Europe because of overcrowded skies. Congested roads add further to the attractiveness of the train as an alternative carrier and we are likely to see the private sector offering integrated transportation packages.

7 Waste management

Rising environmental concerns and the likelihood of a major environmental disaster over the next 10 years could tighten legislation in the procedures governing waste storage, processing and disposal. Companies in this sector would witness a steep change in demand for their services.

8 Media

The worldwide proliferation of satellite and television channels will call for a rapid increase in the production and distribution of content. Existing providers will be catapulted in to a world of interactive multi-media and 24 hr television. All those companies seeking to meet this demand should prosper.

9 Cellular communications

The telephone as we know it today will be transformed by the mass introduction of cellular phones particularly in the newly industrialized countries of the world where the cost of laying copper wire and cable are untenable. Provided these markets offer western companies stable licensing regimes the prospects for growth are unbounded.

10 Employment agencies

Corporations of the world are demanding more flexible employment arrangements from existing and potential employees. The rise in employment agencies as marketing channels for the portfolio worker of tomorrow and as a resource pool for companies to dip into will create many new entrants and a further consolidation of existing providers.

bibliography

1. Yip, George S., *Total Global Strategy*, Prentice-Hall Inc., 1992
2. Petersen, John L., *The Road to 2015*, Waite Group Press, 1994
3. Birchall, David/Lyons, Laurence, *Creating Tomorrow's Organization*, Pitman Publishing, 1995
4. ——, *The East Asian Miracle: Economic Growth and Public Policy*, Oxford University Press, September 1993
5. ——, *The Economist Book of Vital Statistics*, Hutchinson
6. Brown, Richard/DeAnne, Julius, *Is Manufacturing Still Special in The New World Order?*
7. ——, Julius, *Education at a Glance: OECD Indicators*, HMSO
8. ——, OECD, *Tourism Policy and International Tourism in OECD Countries*, 1993
9. Etzioni, Amitai, *The Parenting Deficit*, Demos, London 1993
10. ——, *Population Projections of the United States, by Age, Sex, Race, and Hispanic Origin: 1991 to 2050*, US Department of Commerce, 1992
11. Pearce, Fred, *The Damned Rivers, Dams, and the Coming World Water Crisis*, The Bodley Head, 1992
12. Schwartz, Peter, *The Art of the Long View*, Century Business, 1993
13. Handy, Charles, *The Age of Unreason*, Business Books Limited, 1989
14. ——, *World Nuclear Industry Handbook 1993*
15. McRae, Hamish, *The World in 2020*, Harper Collins Publishers, 1994
16. ——, "It Sounds Terrific Until You Realize Who's Paying For It," *The Wall Street Journal Europe*, October 6–7, 1995
17. ——, "Cyber Trading: A London Institution Sounds the Retreat in High-Tech Conflict," *The Wall Street Journal Europe*, September 29–30, 1995
18. ——, *Social Trends 1995*, HMSO
19. ——, "No Loafing About in the Grain Store," *The Guardian*, September 20, 1995
20. ——, "Cities," *The Economist*, July 19, 1995
21. ——, "Rich Grazing for Food Groups," *Financial Times*, August 21, 1995
22. ——, "Malaysia's Success Softens Trade Blow," *Financial Times*, August 21, 1995
23. ——, "What Makes US Women Voters Cross," *US News and World Report*, August 1995
24. ——, "The Age of Asia: Learning from the Sunrise Societies," *Demos Quarterly* Issue 6, 1995

25. ——, "Business in China," *The American Management Association Magazine*, August 1995

26. ——, "Pharmacia and Upjohn meet in a Marriage of Equals," *Financial Times*, August 21, 1995

27. ——, "The Internet," *The Economist*, July 1, 1995

28. Lansley, Stewart at The Henley Centre, *After the Gold Rush*, Century Business Books, London 1994

29. ——, "Women Winning Battle of the Sexes in the Workplace," *Financial Times*, September 26, 1995

30. Katz, John, "Guilty," *Wired*, September, 1995

31. Gabriel, Yiannis/Lang, Tim, *The Unmanageable Consumer*, Sage, September 1995

32. ——, *Social Focus on Women*, Central Statistical Office, 1995

33. ——, "Cybersickness: The Side Effects of Virtual Reality," *Trends*, July 14, 1995

34. Crook, Clive, "The Future of Capitalism," *150 Economist Years*, 1995

35. Bergsten, Fred C., "The Rationale for a Rosy View," *150 Economist Years*, 1995

36. Kay, John, "Keeping up with the Market," *150 Economist Years*, 1995

37. ——, "The Disappearing Family," *The Economist*, September 9, 1995

38. ——, "Teenage Mothers, Another Home, Another Chance," *The Economist*, September 9, 1995

39. ——, "Trade War Warrior Waits in the Wings," *Financial Times*, September 1995

40. ——, "All at Sea in Cynicism," *Financial Times*, September 8, 1995

41. ——, "DNA Database Matches First Crime Samples," *Daily Telegraph*, August 12, 1995

42. Marr, Andrew, *Ruling Britannia: The Failure and Future of British Democracy*, Michael Joseph, London 1995

43. ——, "The 10 Best Ideas of the Decade: Your Complete Guide," *Independent Section Two*, November 29, 1995

44. ——, "Innovation is the Destination," *Financial Times*, September 18, 1995

45. ——, "Dry Measures: A Question of Water Underlies Relations on Iberian Peninsula," *The Wall Street Journal Europe*, October 26, 1995

46. ——, "Chernobyl's Uncertain Future," *Financial Times*, October 18, 1995

47. ——, "What We Should Do About 'Global Warming'...," *The Wall Street Journal Europe*, October 19, 1995

48. ——, "Boom and Gloom: Despite Rapid Growth of China's Economy, Many are Suffering," *The Wall Street Journal Europe*, October 20, 1995

49. ——, "PCs Take Two Steps Ahead, One Stride Back," *The Wall Street Journal Europe*, October 20, 1995

50. ——, "Is There Life After Reengineering," *Industry Forum*, April 1995

51. ——, "See You in Cybercourt," *Information Management Forum*, April 1995

52. ——, "The Networked Corporation: Linking up is Hard to do – but it's a Necessity," *Business Week*, June 26, 1995
53. ——, "What's on American Managers' Minds," *The American Management Association Magazine*, April 1995
54. ——, "Antagonists Clear the Air," *Financial Times*, September 27, 1995
55. Schwartz, Evan I., "Wanna Bet? At US$40 billion a Year the US Gambling is Already Bigger than Movies and Music Combined. Guess What's Going to be the Real Killer App on the Net?," *Wired*, October 1995
56. ——, "Europe Fails to Curb Summer Smog in Cities," *Financial Times*, October 6, 1995
57. ——, "London Leads Global Currency Markets, Followed by New York, Tokyo, and Singapore," *The Wall Street Journal Europe*, September 20, 1995
58. Barnett, Steve, *The Nissan Report*, Avon Books, 1993
59. Drucker, Peter F., *Managing for the Future*, Butterworth-Heinemann Limited, 1995
60. Davidow, William H./Malone, Michael S., *The Virtual Corporation*, Harper Collins Publishers Inc., 1992
61. Davis, Stan/Davidson, Bill, *2020 Vision*, Fireside, 1991
62. Peppers, Don/Rogers, Martha, *The One-to-One Future*, Judy Piatkus (Publishers) Limited, 1994
63. Naisbitt, John, *Global Paradox*, Nicholas Brealey Publishing Limited, 1994
64. Barnet, Richard J./Cavanagh, John, *Global Dreams*, Touchstone, 1995
65. ——, "Public Distrust of Politicians High, Poll Finds," *Financial Times*, November 23, 1995
66. ——, "Beyond Beijing," *Financial Times*, December 1995
67. ——, "Work is a Four-Letter Word," *Independent*, October 26, 1995
68. ——, "A Responsible Divorce Law," *Independent*, October 1995
69. ——, "Telework: Back to the Future," *Financial Times*, November 22, 1995
70. ——, "Role Model: Teen Tycoon Gives Risk-Averse Germans a Lesson in Survival," *The Wall Street Journal Europe*, January 4, 1996
71. ——, "Shareholder Revolt," *Business Week*, September 18, 1995
72. ——, "Will You be Lonesome Tonight," *Independent Section Two*, October 19, 1995
73. ——, "World Bank Plans $11 bn Fund for Poorest Nations," *Financial Times*, September 14, 1995
74. ——, "China's New Elite," *Business Week*, June 5, 1995
75. ——, "March May Give Farrakhan Wider US Role," *The Wall Street Journal Europe*, October 12, 1995
76. ——, "Good Design Can Counter Data Fraud," *Financial Times Review*, October 4, 1995
77. ——, "Europe's Far Right: Something Nasty in the Woodshed," *The Economist*, October 21, 1995

78. ——, "World Bank Chief Fears Big Cuts by Congress," *Financial Times*, September 22, 1995

79. Rogers, Paul/Dando, Malcolm, "Conflict, Development and North–South Relations – Trends in Global Security After the Cold War," Annual Conference, University of Lancaster, September 7–9, 1994

80. Rogers, Paul, "Development, Environment and International Security," Department of Peace Studies, Bradford University, April 6–8, 1995

81. ——, "The Age of Asia: Learning from the Sunrise Societies," *Demos* Issue 6, 1995

82. ——, "The Berlusconi of the Net," *Wired*, November 1995

83. ——, "A Strong Urge to Join the Club," *Financial Times*, October 6, 1995

84. ——, "Water: Flowing Uphill," *The Economist*, August 12, 1995

85. ——, "Seers in a Slump: As Firms Cut Back, Business Economists Find Jobs Dwindling: Some Seek a Direct Impact on Profits; Others Try Consulting or Newsletters," *The Wall Street Journal Europe*, October 9, 1995

86. ——, "The Myth of the Powerless State," *The Economist*, October 7, 1995

87. ——, "Two Nations, Divisible: the Intolerable Lesson on the O.J. Simpson Trial," *The Economist*, October 7, 1995

88. ——, "Ageing Problem Upsets Government Calculations," *Financial Times*, October 6, 1995

89. ——, "Seize the Initiative: Individuals Must Take Responsibility for their Careers," *Financial Times*, October 9, 1995

90. Maxwell, Robert J., "Rationing Health Care," Churchill Care

91. ——, "Struggle to Jump Green Barriers," *Financial Times*, October 26, 1995

92. ——, "They Have Nine TV Sets, Six Computers, Three Cars and Every Domestic Appliance. What Would Life be Like Without Them?," *Daily Telegraph*, October 26, 1995

93. ——, "Of Course the Rich are Much Healthier," *Daily Telegraph*, October 1995

94. ——, "So Where Were You Last Monday, Sisters?," *The Guardian*, October 23, 1995

95. ——, "Age of the Cool Nerd," *The Guardian*, October 1995

96. ——, "The West Will Lose its Grip on the World," *Independent on Sunday*, October 8, 1995

97. ——, "Freedom's Children," *Demos*, 1995

98. ——, "The West Embarks on Long March to a Low-Wage World," *Financial Times*, September 21, 1995

99. Peterson, Wallace C., *Silent Depression: Twenty-Five Years of Wage Squeeze and Middle Class Decline*, WW Norton & Co.

100. ——, "Buddha's Booming," *The Guardian*, October 4, 1995

101. ——, "UK Brewer Scores with Neo-Bass-ical Pubs," *The Wall Street Journal*, October 4, 1995

102. ——, "Enthusiasm Cools for Debt Relief Proposal," *Financial Times*, October 4, 1995
103. ——, "America and O.J. Simpson," *Financial Times*, October 4, 1995
104. Marris, Robin, "Growth is the Best Way to Reduce Social Dislocation," *The Times*, October 3, 1995
105. Gingrich, Newt, *To Renew America*, Harper Collins
106. ——, "Planning for the Virtual Enterprise: The Changing World of Work," The Strategic Planning Society & Henley Management College – A One-Day Conference, 1995

appendix

"Hold-up"

A short play by Bill Cashmore on the two-tier world scenario

*Two terrorists (one male, one female), dressed in khakis, bandanas, etc,
enter explosively. They have weapons and are threatening.*

FEMALE: Shut up!

MALE: Nobody move!

FEMALE: Stay exactly where you are!

MALE: If anybody tries to leave, I'll detonate the 200 kg of explosives hidden in this room.

FEMALE: Enough explosives to destroy The Dorchester and most of Mayfair.

MALE: So sit very still.

FEMALE: And keep very quiet.

MALE: OK. Now let's introduce ourselves and tell you why we're here.

FEMALE: We are the advance task force of the year 2015 Lo-ed Terrorist Group.

MALE: Our aim is to redress the appalling imbalance between ourselves, the lo-eds, and you, the alrights.

FEMALE: And we can make a start today by relieving you of all your items of importance and value.

MALE: So when we finally let you leave this room, deposit all your gold timepieces, jewellery, Intersmart cards, vehicle microchips, and items of a personal nature with us. An infra-red detector will detect anybody who tries to leave this room with anything of importance. So be warned.

FEMALE: Now, this visit to the heartland of the alrights by the 2015 Lo-ed Terrorist Group is the beginning of our campaign to show that the pathetic attempts of the alrights to protect themselves from the rest of the world will never succeed.

MALE: You may have money and power but we have organization and belief, and something you will never have, humanity.

FEMALE: So listen very closely to our demands for a world where the sickening gap between the haves and have-nots is closed once and for all.

MALE: [*Producing piece of paper*] And as we speak be aware that the Internet has been totally hijacked and that these demands are simultaneously appearing at workstations around the world.

FEMALE: Homes. We demand the complete cessation of future building of metaloplastic "iggies" and the destruction of all those that have been built. These so-called homes are degrading and unfit for human habitation. We also demand the demolition of the uninhabitable estates built at the end of the last century. We will enforce the building of quality homes for all.

MALE: Schools. We demand an end to all privileged private education. All our state schools should be places of understanding, care, and nourishment and not places of anger and aggression peopled by armed guards. We demand that teachers return to work in these schools to replace the uneducated warders and protection units. The world needs education. For all.

FEMALE: Shops and services. We demand access to a full range of goods and services, and not the leftovers and scraps from the alrights. We have a right to shop anywhere and should not need special identification or Intersmart cards to enter Shop Till 'U Drop malls. The food we eat should be of the same quality worldwide for all.

[*Zadok the priest – Handel's coronation theme – can be heard faintly in the background, but as the demands continue it becomes increasingly prominent.*]

MALE: Life. Everyone has the right to preserve his or her own life. We demand an end to privileged healthcare, compulsory euthanasia, and enforced genocide based on meritocratic testing. We insist on health for all.

FEMALE: The family unit. This is flexible and should be treated as such. It is unreasonable to expect lifetime cohabitation. Movement between family units should be rewarded and encouraged, not penalized and scorned. Freedom of parenthood for all.

MALE: Mobility. Abolish all no-go areas. The protected havens and enclaves of the alrights must be dismantled. We must learn to live in multinational and multicultural settlements everywhere. A free world for all.

FEMALE: Because, at present, you get rich and fat. When you retire, you've got something for your old age, and something for your kids. What have we got? Nothing. Our health is ruined and we're thrown onto the rubbish tip and onto charity.

MALE: Our aim is to make the world a place where our kids won't come to want.

[*Blackout and music comes to abrupt stop.*]

index

7493